MOIRA SHEPARD

Love Your Way to Success

FIVE KEYS TO CONFIDENCE FOR CREATIVE WOMEN ENTREPRENEURS

Love Your Way to Success

Five Keys to Confidence for Creative Women Entrepreneurs

To Vicki, the best sister ever.

Pick Up Your Free Confidence-Building Playbook

If you want to start turning your dream business into a successful and satisfying enterprise, get your free copy of "3 Power Moves to Share Your Gifts with the World: Your Confidence-Building Playbook."

The act of sharing your gifts creates a profound level of self-assurance. It builds dynamic confidence that carries you forward.

In this fun, easy guidebook you will find:

- The secret to building confidence you can count on
- Inspiration to get your creative juices flowing
- Fun, simple ways to get your gifts out there

Pick up your free guidebook to help you get on track—and stay there—at http://www.confidencebuildingplaybook.com today.

To your success!
Moira Shepard

Testimonials

"Moira Shepard is a marvel and so is her book, *Love Your Way to Success!* Filled with amazing and life-changing stories, she shows you the path to self-confidence and love she walked herself. You'll fall in love with her—and yourself-along the way. A terrific guide for growing into your best self and owning your power!"

—*Chellie Campbell, author* The Wealthy Spirit
and From Worry to Wealthy

"Moira, you haven't just solved my problem—you've changed my life!"
—*Arjang Zendehdel, Pacific Palisades, CA*

"I've gotten more out of one hour with Moira than everything I've done in the past three years!"
—*Janet Nicholson, Los Angeles, CA*

"I felt immediately that Moira is totally invested in helping me have my best life possible and have it easily and NOW. My session with her, while felt and tangible immediately, had a lasting effect in my life. I cannot recommend Moira enough. If you have an issue you want to shift now or just move to the next level of love in your life, work with Moira. You will be so grateful you did."
—*Eric Fricke, Santa Fe, NM*

"All I can say is WOW!!! From the deepest, truest part of myself, thank you! You have aided me in such an incredibly astounding and amazing fashion that, looking only from a vantage point of a mere three days from then, I am already feeling an astonishingly immense amount of who I truly am is finally coming to the surface!"
—*Brian Daniel Billie, Idaho Falls, ID*

Contents

Acknowledgments   **8**

Preface   **11**

Introduction   **26**
If your confidence comes and goes like the tide, this book is for you.

Confidence Key #1 – Master Your Mind   **37**
You can guide your mind to create a successful and soul-satisfying business.

Confidence Key #2 – Honor Your Heart   **53**
You can handle your feelings, so they work for you instead of against you.

Confidence Key #3 – Respect Your Body   **63**
You can discover fun and unexpected ways to care for your body as if it were a treasure. It is.

Confidence Key #4 – Cherish Your Spirit   **80**
You can tap into and direct the power within you, with confidence and joy.

Confidence Key #5 – Serve the Greater Good   **103**
You can share your gifts in a way that blesses others, as well as yourself.

Afterword   **123**
You are part of the glorious tribe of humanity's creators, innovators, and visionaries.

Acknowledgments

This book has been made possible by a number of people who deserve my heartfelt appreciation.

My family, who have been my greatest teachers. My pioneer ancestors, the giants on whose shoulders I stand.

Longtime friends Kelley Wright, my precious soul sister; and Chanda Counts, my dear sister traveler on the path. You have helped me in so many ways; it's impossible to name them all.

My former colleagues at Times Mirror Magazines, who took the time to encourage me to be more: Granville Swope, Owen Buckley, Jim Kahn, Jim Mahoney, Mary McGrath, Richard Katz, Ron Riemer, Larry Wondero, Renett Goree and Rosina Pennacchio. It took me years to act on your wise counsel, but I got there, thanks—in large part—to you.

Master healers of soaring genius who have honored me with their friendship and support: Master Theta Healer Karen Abrams; Breathwork master Maren Nelson; Healer, author and thought leader Emmanuel Dagher; Soul Mastery expert Susann Taylor Shier; Angel and Akashic Reader Tricia Ebert; Healer, author and speaker Brent Phillips; and chiropractic magician Dr. Steve Scully. I give thanks every day for the presence of these angels in my life.

The gifted healers who helped me recover from a back injury that kept me bedridden for seven years: David Bingham Fox, C.H.T.; chiropractor Steve Scully, D.C.; energy healers Satish Dholakia and Susanna Horton; distance healer Candis Ross; angel reader Kalie Noelle; transformational psychologist Dr. Meg Haworth; as well as my medical teams at UCLA Medical Center, Centinela Hospital and Kerlan-Jobe Orthopaedic Clinic. You gave me help and hope when I felt I had nowhere to turn. Bless you!

The many brilliant mentors, teachers, and trainers who have given me the benefit of their skill and wisdom: Rockhouse Global Founder Christopher Howard; Dreamality Education & Coaching Founder Arjang Zendehdel and his wonderful community; Angel Therapy ® Founder and author Doreen Virtue; Chellie Cambell, Financial Stress Reduction Expert and author of *The Wealthy Spirit*; Theta Healing ® Founder Vianna Stibal; the late, great Theta Healer Terry O'Connell; Radiance Technique ® Master Joyce Kenyon; Millionaire Mind master T. Harv Eker; Akashic Records masters Linda Howe and Barbara Schiffman; One Command ® Founder Asara Lovejoy; speaking coach Jack Barnard; multi-dimensional healer Dr. Kathleen Lewis; Sacred Geometry master Samuel Kiwasz; Rev. James E. Daly; and dearly departed healer Nicole Pigeault. You have done me the greatest service one person can do for another: you helped me remember who I really am.

The awe-inspiring women who showed me how to leap out of my comfort zone and become a heart-centered entrepreneur: Dating Director Cherry Norris, enlightened entrepreneur, mastermind buddy, and cherished friend; Christine Kloser, whose spiritual approach to entrepreneurship awakened me and countless others to what is possible; fantastic Feng Shui practitioner and indefatigable entrepreneur P.K. Odle; Alexandria Brown, a shining star who continues to inspire me; brilliant business leader Melanie Benson Strick; red-hot copywriter Lorrie Morgan; branding genius Kim Castle; business mentor Baeth Davis; Commanding Wealth Coach Kathryn Perry; Financial Alchemist Morgana Rae; Love and Relationship expert Rori Raye; inspired healing center Founders Rev. Danielle Marie Hewitt (Temple of Light) and Avghi Constantinides (Los Angeles Centre for Life); online radio pioneer Linda Mackenzie (HealthyLife.net); Man Whisperer and writing mentor Donna Sozio; Santa Monica Aura Shop owner Kate Mitchell; writing mentor Joanna Penn of The Creative Penn; and Speaker Services founder Susan Levin, who now guides me from above, bless her. The creativity, passion, and professionalism of these women inspires me every day.

My dearly beloved clients, followers, listeners, viewers, radio show guests, readers, and students have given me far more than I ever gave them. Thank you for allowing me to serve you. You are shining stars and I adore you. You know who you are.

The telesummit hosts and producers who invited me to share my message, helping me to realize how many people could be helped by this information: Darius Barazandeh; Debra Poneman; Eram Saeed; Moncef

Afkir; Judy Anderson; Alicia Ashley; Jim Beach; Alara Canfield; Danielle Fitzpatrick Clark; Emmanuel Dagher; Denise Dominguez; Sue Fellows; JJ Flizanes; Lance Hood; Cindy Kubica; Melissa LeBlanc; Michelle Lee; Ed Lester; Jane Lorenz; Maureen Mongrain; Sarah Ouelette; Sheldon Pizzinat; Mel Robertson; Dr. Linda Sanicola; Elizabeth Scheffer; and radio show hosts April Cline, Diane A. Curran, Linda Koss and Kristin Macdonald. Your work supports the magnificence of millions of people. Much love and many blessings to you!

Many sages of the ages have inspired me from the moment I read the story of Joan of Arc as a child, revealing a life lived with faith and courage that lit up my soul. Reading the heartwarming and uplifting works of Louisa May Alcott led me to Transcendentalists like Ralph Waldo Emerson and Henry David Thoreau. I went on to study the New and Old Testaments; the Kabbalah; the works of Lao Tzu; the teachings of Gautama Buddha; the Tao te Ching; the Bhagavad Gita; the Course in Miracles; "Science of Mind" and other New Thought works by Ernest Holmes; "Game of Life" author Florence Scovel Shinn; as well as the works of masterful contemporary authors like Marianne Williamson, Wayne Dyer, Anne Lamott, Thich Nhat Hanh, Martha Beck, the Dalai Lama, Louise Hay, Gregg Braden, Carolyn Myss, Bruce Lipton, Cheryl Richardson, Tama Kieves, Mark Nepo, Tara Brach, Rev. Dr. Jesse Jennings, Matthew Alper, Geneen Roth, Dr. Daniel Amen, Dr. Candace Pert, and Dr. Eben Alexander; my favorite physicist, Carlo Rovelli, and my favorite neuroscientist, Dr. Andrew Newberg. Our bodies may perish, but great thoughts live forever. Thank you for sharing your wisdom. You grace us all.

Last, yet far from least, a big shout-out to brilliant book coach Donna Kozik, who helped me shape and finish this book. Many thanks, dear Donna, to you and your terrific team!

Preface

If you're like me, you weren't born confident. Quite the opposite. So, if I can develop confidence that's authentic and consistent, so can you.

Before I show you how to do it, let me tell you how I did it. It's a story that involves back pain, miraculous healings, and a life more fulfilling than I ever dreamed possible.

Come and walk with me for a bit

Pain woke me up out of a sound sleep at about 3 a.m. on April 1, 1997. It felt like a jackhammer jabbing into my spine. The pain shocked me. I tried to shift my position and got a bigger shock. I couldn't move. Not a finger. Not a toe. My body was a jail.

I panicked. I started to cry but realized I could drown in my own snot if I didn't stop. So, I breathed as deeply as I could to calm down.

While breathing, I reviewed the day in my mind to see if I could figure out what brought this on.

It had been the final day of a mailing project. It concluded with temps presenting me with three 50-pound boxes to go down to the mailroom.

I picked up the first box and headed out of the office. Carrying a 50-pound box was no big deal. As a gym rat for the last twenty years, I hefted more weight than that every day.

The magazines shifted as I walked toward the elevator. I rocked back on my spine a bit as I rebalanced the weight. I felt a little -snick- in my lower spine, but that was all. Two more 50-pound trips to the mailroom completed the project without further incident.

At quitting time, I drove home to my apartment in Venice, California. Then I walked the four blocks to my favorite beach hangout. No friends were there that evening, so I sat alone, drinking in the sunset and a Guinness.

Sitting started to feel uncomfortable. I left my drink half-finished and walked home. It was about 6:30 p.m.—early for me but lying down was all I could think about.

I went home and went to sleep until this pain woke me up.

When panic tapered off into exhaustion, I found that if I took it a millimeter at a time, I could move. It took several hours to crawl from my bed to the desk phone in the living room to summon help.

Once at the desk, I couldn't reach the phone from the floor. I inched toward the phone cord on the carpet and pulled it until the phone fell off the desk and onto the floor near me. My hands shook so much, it took several tries to call for help.

While the phone rang on the other side, questions bubbled up in my brain. What's up with this pain? How can I work? I can barely move. Right now, I can't even put on a pair of pants.

My worst fears come true

With no work, no mobility, and no pants, I drifted through a year...then another year...and another. All told, I spent seven years in bed, only leaving home to see doctors, get tests, have surgeries, and do physical therapy. In case you're counting, that's 2,557 days or 3,681,785 minutes. I aged from 39 to 46. It gives a person a lot of time to think.

The time slipped by while I was bombed out of my mind on Vicodin, plus assorted non-narcotic painkillers and anti-inflammatories. Enough pills to sink a battleship … but not enough to give me back my life.

My brain felt like cotton candy. My body felt like a lump of pain, with just enough life force to keep me alive.

But I didn't care. That's what opiates do for you. They don't stop the pain. They make you indifferent to your own suffering. If I was depressed or anxious, I was too medicated to notice it.

After four years and five failed surgeries, I grew impatient with the daily routine of coaxing my aching body out of bed each morning and trudging to the kitchen to take the first of four daily doses of opiates.

Laying down on the daybed to rest and watch "Perry Mason" if I felt up to following a storyline.

Watching the sky from the picture window near the daybed.

Trying to assemble breakfast (granola and yogurt), lunch (soup), and dinner (more soup) while clutching the kitchen countertop for support.

Balancing a bowl of food on my chest while lying on the daybed, since it hurt too much to sit up and eat.

Swallowing one last dose of Vicodin before crawling into bed, exhausted and hurting.

Good times.

Living alone, I could never have managed without the generous assistance of friends and family.

My father drove me to nearly every doctor appointment, surgery, and physical therapy appointment over the course of seven years. My mother drove 100 miles round trip every week to bring groceries and do my laundry. My sister Vicki called every afternoon, so I could hear at least one live human voice every day. Friends occasionally came by with treats and kindly took out the trash when they left. My friend Kelley took care of me at her family's home for two weeks when a surgery left me too debilitated to go home. Kelley's father, Bob, saved my life by driving me to the emergency room when a massive blood clot developed. My aunt Marguerite took care of me in her home for three months when the blood clot rendered my left leg incapable of supporting my weight: it collapsed whenever I tried to stand up.

I felt beyond blessed to have such kind people in my life. It was humbling to realize how many people cared about me.

All the same, I got tired of living the life of a sickly 85-year-old woman while still in my 40s.

So, while lying on the examination table at my doctor's office in January 2001, I took a deep breath and steeled myself to ask my doctor a question (even though I wasn't sure I wanted to know the answer):

"Is this going to be my life? Staring at four walls all day long and coming to see you once a month?"

The doctor looked me steadily as he softly said, "Look, we fused your spine. There's nothing left to do." He opened his hands with an air of resignation. "Surgically, you're at the end of the road."

My mind went blank. I couldn't take it in. I didn't cry. Didn't talk. I was in shock.

On automatic pilot, I rolled off the examination table. My stepmother Diana, who drove me to the doctor's office for that particular check-up, pushed my wheelchair toward me and watched carefully to make sure I got settled into it. Somehow, she knew I needed silence right then.

We drove home without saying anything. It felt as if a touch or a word would shatter me into a million pieces. Diana, ever compassionate and intuitive, let me know by her warm presence that she was there for me. That was all I could take in. And it was all I needed at that moment. Bless her.

She carried my fold-up wheelchair up the 27 steps to my apartment, following behind me to make sure I got up the stairs okay. Once through the front door, I went straight to the daybed and lay down. Diana tucked a blanket over me and kissed me on the forehead.

"Call me if you want to talk," she said, and left.

I closed my eyes. The conversation with the doctor replayed in my mind over and over. I sank deeper into despair by the moment. I was never, ever, going to get better. My stomach hollowed out at the thought.

When it felt like I hit the bottom of blackness, a small voice within me spoke words that would change my life.

It said, "Thank you for sharing. I'm going to go and get well now."

"Thank you for sharing. I'm going to go and get well now."

The voice felt true and real. I wanted to believe it. Could there really be light at the end of this tunnel? Would I have a life beyond these four walls someday?

I had come to hate hope because disappointment always seemed to follow in its wake. But this voice activated in me something deeper than hope. It awakened faith. Not faith in myself—I felt too helpless and hopeless for that—but faith that life wanted me to get better. That more was waiting for me. That I wasn't done.

I didn't know how or when I would get well. But it felt like something wiser than me had made its presence known. I would leave my recovery in its hands.

A turning point

Sometime later, my father suggested trying out a hypnotherapist he knew who specialized in helping people with chronic pain like mine.

At first, I was skeptical. It sounded pretty woo-woo to me. But maybe this was a sign from the universe to look beyond conventional Western medicine. What did I have to lose?

I felt nervous on the day of the appointment. My father and I sat in patient silence in the waiting room, wondering what to expect, and yet expecting nothing.

In our session, David Bingham Fox (now retired) asked what brought me to him.

I told him, "I've spent the last five years in bed because it hurts too much to sit, stand, or walk."

In his deep baritone, he explained how hypnosis worked. He thought he could help me. He assured me he would do his best.

David began by leading me through a guided meditation that left me feeling deeply relaxed, but still conscious.

At one point he said, "Picture your brain as a control room."

The command deck of the starship *Enterprise* came to mind. No sign of Captain Kirk or Mr. Spock. This was my domain.

"Imagine the control panel has a dial with the numbers one through ten on it," David instructed. "On a scale of one to ten, what level is your pain right now?"

"It's at seven," I whispered.

"See the dial pointing at seven. Now turn it up to eight."

To my shock, the pain instantly intensified.

"Now turn it down to three."

More shockingly, the pain eased.

"Now turn it up to five."

The pain shot back up to level five.

"Now turn it down to one."

The pain vanished.

Oh, my gosh. The pain *vanished*.

It seemed unbelievable. Yet, it had happened. I didn't know what to think. A warm rush of emotion flooded my heart. Soft tears of relief and gratitude rolled down my cheeks.

"Are you okay there?" he asked.

"Yes. Yes. I'm just … amazed."

David slowly brought me back to full consciousness. I felt relaxed yet alert, and free of pain.

"Saying 'thank you' seems so inadequate," I said. "But thank you."

He smiled. "I'm just glad I could help. Let me know how it goes, will you? You're welcome to come back any time."

We shook hands, and I slowly walked out into the waiting room to meet my father. He smiled with relief when he saw my face. I was glowing.

"So, it went well?"

"Oh, yes! I want to come back again next week."

"Let's set it up right now."

I called my doctor as soon as I got home, to ask for a taper-down program to get off narcotic painkillers. I hated taking those pills. Thank goodness I was only physically addicted to opiates, not emotionally.

With the help of hypnotherapist David and my doctor, I was narcotic-free within three months. David and I worked together weekly for nine months after that.

By then, I could sit, stand, and walk for up to 15 minutes a day. This was huge. But I ached to be productive again after years of feeling like a useless lump.

Starting my first business

Fortunately, the internet happened while I was away. Within months, I launched an online copywriting business from my daybed. It was so much fun, creating content for websites and print ads. I still could barely sit, stand, or walk because my muscles had atrophied after years of disuse. But my clients never knew that. All our consultations happened by phone or email.

The new business led to meeting other entrepreneurs to socialize, share business tips, and refer clients to each other at Christine Kloser's spiritual networking group, N.E.W. Entrepreneurs. They met in Santa Monica, half a mile from my apartment. Perfect for my limited driving range, but even more perfect because of the brilliant, insightful, soulful women I met there, starting with Christine herself.

Although the decreased pain made it possible for me to leave the house and drive a short distance, I still brought a fold-up chaise to these gatherings because I couldn't sit through a three-hour meeting. It must have been quite a sight to see me stretched out on a lounge chair as if I were waiting for someone to bring me a margarita, but I didn't care. I wanted to be there.

One day at a networking meeting, speaker Christopher Howard talked about how changing your mind can change your life.

He put us all in a trance and gave us a post-hypnotic suggestion: over the next seven days, we would wake up with three million-dollar ideas. Just the thing for ambitious entrepreneurs like us.

I went to sleep that cold night of November 20, 2003, with difficulty. I was excited to find out what my first million-dollar idea would be.

A calling

A sound wakes me up. I feel scared. Did an intruder break in? Venice isn't the safest neighborhood in the world.

Frightened, I forget how to breathe for a moment. There's the sound again. I listen harder. It's soft at first, then it gets louder. It sounds like singing. It sounds like … *angels*?

A chorus of loving voices says, "Moira, wake up."

"I'm up," I say.

"We need you. It's time for you to get out of bed and heal the world. GET UP!"

I roll out of bed and stagger to my feet. Lean on the bed for support. Shiver with cold and fear.

"Who are you?" I say. "Where are you?"

I want to snap on the bedside lamp to see better, but the room already looks filled with light. At 3:30 in the morning.

The light resolves into visions. I see myself speaking in front of thousands of eager listeners. I'm there to heal the world. I'm a leader. People look at me. I look at them. My voice is loud and clear. My body is healthy and strong. I'm touching the hearts of these people, encouraging them, loving them. Something brought us together, and I am there to inspire them with my story.

The visions go on for hours. Dawn comes and goes without my noticing as I scribble page upon page of notes.

I ask questions: "Does this mean I have to give up everything and live in an ashram in India or something?"

"You can if you want to," comes the reply. "But you can work just as well from where you are right now."

"Why me?"

"This is what you came here to do."

The visions light up my soul. The voices fill me with courage and hope. That day, I dedicate my life to this calling.

Do I have confidence that I can heal myself or others? Nope. Not even a little bit.

Do I believe in this calling? Yes. With all my heart.

Do I trust that whatever called me would never lure me out on a limb and then saw it off behind me? Yes. Inexplicably, utterly, yes.

I have no idea what to do or how to do it. I only know one thing: I am going to do it.

I have no idea what to do or how to do it.
I only know one thing: I am going to do it.

For the rest of the day, I think about where to start in practical terms. First things first. If I'm going to help people to heal, I have to be completely healed myself.

Another day, another miracle

I began by studying with Christopher Howard, the speaker and trainer whose talk set the stage for my miraculous awakening. It meant taking on debt, but if I was going to follow my calling, it was necessary to learn how to heal.

Confirmation that I was on the right track came just two days into my three-week NLP, hypnotherapy, and speaker training program with Christopher.

On the first day, 10 hours of sitting made my spine feel like it was on fire.

On the second day, the back pain burned deeper. I felt frustrated with my body and worried that I would never get through the remainder of the training.

But on that day, we learned about pain specialist Dr. John Sarno's claim that if you've had proper treatment for your injury and you still have pain six weeks later, the source of the pain is emotional or mental rather than physical.

Hmmmm. That got me thinking. I was living life and loving it. But my spinal nerves felt inflamed from so much sitting, and my last surgery was four years ago. A lot longer than six months.

As soon as I got home, I lay down on the daybed to have a little chat with my spine about what was going on.

"Hello, spine," I said. "What's up with the pain?" I took care to use a tone of curiosity, as if I were conducting a science experiment. Didn't want to scare my spine by interrogating it like a district attorney.

To my surprise, a childish voice answered. "You've had a very hard time. You've struggled all your life. We're keeping you safe in bed, so you won't have to try so hard anymore."

I thought about that. It sounded pretty reasonable, in an unreasonable sort of way.

"Tell you what," I said. "I want to be safe too. We want the same thing here. Does it make sense to you that I would be safer if I were healthy and strong instead of weak and debilitated?"

A long pause followed. Finally, the voice shyly confessed, "I never thought of that."

One minute later, the burning back pain went away. It shook me, how quickly the pain vanished. Sort of like Dorothy in "The Wizard of Oz," finding out her ruby slippers could have taken her home at any time. But my first attempt at self-healing worked; the pain never came back.

Seeing firsthand the effectiveness of intuitive and mental healing techniques, I continued learning and using them to heal myself. It seemed like the best first step in getting out there and doing my part to heal the world. Who would trust a healer capable of standing for only 15 minutes a day? Not me, and probably not you. Rightly so.

Most of the trainings included working on my fellow trainees to practice the skills we were learning. At every training, at least one trainee—and often my instructor, as well—would tell me I should hang out my shingle as a practitioner.

Even so, I kept putting off the day when I would offer my services as a healing professional.

Getting out there

Instead, I offered myself as a public speaker. I felt more confident talking about healing than doing it on other people, despite the successful sessions I'd conducted as a trainee.

I outlined my first talk by asking myself, "What are three things that people need to know about healing?" and wrote a signature speech from there: "Three Steps to Triumph Over Trauma."

Avghi Constantinedes, the founder of Centre for Life in Culver City, generously invited me to give the talk at her center.

I felt nervous as the day approached. I'd gotten in front of people as an actress, back when dinosaurs ruled the Earth, but never as myself. Would my talk put people to sleep? Would I be good enough?

Before the starting time, I blessed the empty room and all who would enter it. People started coming in … and more … and more. More than 30 people packed one small room to listen to an unknown woman talk about healing, of all things.

I took a deep breath, said a silent prayer, and started talking. Some listeners smiled and nodded. Others had tears in their eyes. Every person looked attentive and interested.

One woman stood up at the end and said, "You are an angel of light! I am so happy I came here to listen to you today!"

I walked over to her. Took her hands in mine. Looked into her eyes. And said, "You couldn't see that light in me unless you are an angel, too. We're angels together. All of us!" We embraced. Applause and cheers filled the room.

More invitations to speak came in. And Linda Mackenzie, founder of HealthyLife.net, recruited me to host a show on her online radio network. We decided to call it "Triumph Over Trauma."

A radio veteran, Linda had a full production studio set up in her El Segundo home. I drove there every week to talk with guests found through networking and word of mouth. My background as a journalist served me well as a radio interviewer, but it took a full month to get over my fear of the microphone. I did it by focusing on my guest, rather than my anxiety.

For nearly three years, I enjoyed the privilege of sharing remarkable stories of courageous people who triumphed over challenges ranging from bankruptcy to cancer to divorce.

It was beyond inspiring to hear Chellie Campbell hilariously describe her path from wannabe actress to best-selling author, world-class speaker, and financial workshop leader. To listen to Lorrie Kazan sharing her moving story of how she came to be one of the top 10 psychics in the world, according to the Edgar Cayce Institute. To marvel at Karen Abrams learning how to heal her debilitating anxiety on the way to becoming a powerful Master Theta Healer.

Once in a while, a guest would pull a no-show, and I would have to fill an hour of airtime by myself. On those occasions, I conducted intuitive healings on the air by connecting with the collective consciousness of my audience to find out what they needed help with that day. It taught me to trust my intuition. I just needed to let my Higher Power do the driving.

If it had been a live show, I would have had callers phone in with their problems. I've done many live call-ins since then on telesummits, podcasts, radio, and online workshops, as well as conducting group healings at talks around town.

I just needed to let my Higher Power
do the driving.

At that time, I felt more comfortable working with groups for free or by donation than with paid private clients one-on-one. I kept putting off the day when I would hang out my shingle as a full-time professional healer.

I wasn't good enough yet.

I didn't know enough yet.

I needed to work with more people for free before I could charge money for this work.

I needed to get another certification ... and another ... and, wait, there's no way I can get out there without adding *this* modality to my toolkit ...

This procrastination landed me deep in debt at insane interest rates.

It cost tens of thousands of dollars in income I could have made if I had started sooner.

Worst of all, I could have helped thousands more people.

Going pro

After a three-month training during the summer of 2006—and nearly fainting over the subsequent credit card charges—I decided it was time to begin taking on paying clients. If three solid years of training and more than a thousand hours of practice weren't enough to qualify me for the work, I would just have to learn by doing it.

Some clients came through word of mouth. Others were referred by my networking friends.

I had been sending out a weekly electronic newsletter called *Miracle Minute*, featuring 60-second healings. All you had to do was read the suggested healing and say "Yes" out loud if you wanted to receive it, and you got it. I'd never heard of anyone offering intuitive healings via email, but the idea wouldn't leave me alone until I acted on it. The experience helped me to wrap my mind around the idea that if I can imagine it, I can do it.

When I placed an offer of private sessions at the bottom of the newsletter, readers started booking appointments with me.

Within two years, I was making twice as much money as I'd made in corporate media. I moved to a spacious two-bedroom apartment in Marina del Rey with a view of the channel. When I looked up from my desk, boats would be sailing by. It was the first place I had ever lived that I absolutely loved.

Comes the crash

Suddenly, it all went kaput. My income evaporated.

Part of it was the economy—the crash in 2008 caught up with me in 2010.

Other parts:

"Shoulding" on myself—I was creating classes I believed I ought to teach, rather than because I felt inspired to offer them. It seemed like good customer service to follow up one popular online course with another that provided the next steps. But my soul rebelled against it: "This isn't what I came here to do!" I had forgotten who I was and what I'd been called to do.

Burnout—I loved my work and completely gave myself over to it. I ran on an unsustainable high. A crash was inevitable.

Lack of life balance—Looking back, it seemed like there was an unlimited source of energy, but mine wasn't getting renewed. I gave all of myself to my work. All I was getting back was money, which was great, but I needed other things, too. My social life was nil. My love life, nonexistent. I hardly saw my family, even though they lived close by. Every event I attended was for work rather than play. I was on a mission, and nothing could be allowed to distract me.

My finances got to the point where my rent had to be paid by credit card. It became clear I had to leave the home I loved.

I spent the next 10 months living in other people's back bedrooms. I felt scared, ashamed, and humiliated. Here was the abundance teacher living in a rented 9x12 room. Talk about not walking your talk. Ouch.

Most of my possessions had to be given away or donated because there was no space for them. Beautiful leather boots, top-of-the-line cookware, hundreds of beloved books—all gone.

Self-doubt started eating me alive. Given the crash of my business, I had to ask myself, "Have I been teaching lies? Have I been deluding myself? Have I been deluding others?" The idea that I might have unwittingly led other people astray shredded my heart into little pieces.

Prayer and reflection brought me to the conclusion that I had been speaking and teaching truth as I understood it. With all my heart, I believe that love is the greatest healing power in the universe. That by using universal laws and principles, anyone can find their way home to wholeness. That the Higher Power of your understanding wants for you what you want for yourself.

So, if God wanted me to be successful, there must be something in me that had sabotaged my success. What could it be?

Part of it was that I hit my financial glass ceiling, so the excess money— and the things I'd bought with it—had to go because I had "too much." I unconsciously placed limits where, in truth, Infinite Abundance has no ceiling. For you, for me, or for anyone.

Part of it was that it felt weird to make so much money from something that came out of thin air—nothing tangible. I lost sight of the real healing, comfort, and personal growth that people gained—and continue to gain— from my work.

And part of it was the exhaustion. Every cell in my body felt drained. I'd been driving myself without letup since the day of my miraculous awakening; running to keep up with the calling that beckoned me forward. I had no concept then, as I do now, of balance. Of paying attention to other areas of my life. Of honoring my heart, mind, body, and spirit, as well as my call to service. I had an "all or nothing" mentality.

Turning it around

Using my own techniques and working with other healers, I began peeling away the layers of "give until it bleeds" programming I'd carried all my life. I started to perk up again. Things began to change. More money came in.

A small inheritance made it possible to rent a modest apartment of my own. It felt glorious to have all that space to myself. I moved in with only a few shirts, pants and skirts; four pairs of shoes; a computer; and a few books (for me, it's not home unless there are books). Nothing to sit on, cook with, eat off of, or sleep on. I set about furnishing my small kingdom with a grateful heart.

Once I acquired a chair, I sat down to talk with Guidance.

"Maybe it would be easier if I just found a job," I said. "Being an entrepreneur takes a lot of time and energy."

I made the suggestion because I felt scared about money. Frankly, the thought of working in an office filled me with dismay. Not that there is anything wrong with work of that nature. It just wasn't *my* work. Not anymore

"Put getting a job right out of your mind," Guidance replied. "You will never forgive yourself if you turn your back on your work."

It was true. I loved my work, loved being of service, loved seeing the face of a client glowing with new insight and awareness. There was no going back to the little life I led before my back injury.

"Do you really want to withhold your talents from the world?" Guidance asked. "There are people out there who will only accept a healing if it comes from you. There are those who can only understand certain words of wisdom if they are spoken or written by you."

That humbled me. Who was I to play small? Who was I to turn away from so clear a calling?

I made a fresh commitment to my calling and my business. Guidance gave me a clearer understanding that—while I cannot and should not try to heal the world all by myself—there is healing that is mine to do.

My path has taken me here—to you. Come and walk with me for a little while.

Introduction

Begin doing what you want to do now. We are not living in eternity. We have only this moment, sparkling like a star in our hand—and melting like a snowflake

—Francis Bacon

If you're like many creative women, your confidence comes and goes like the tide. Some days it's in full flood. Some days it's out. Some days it's not even on the horizon.

So, if you're looking to create or expand a business based on your creativity, it's essential to cultivate confidence you can count on. Confidence that will lift you up on the good days and support you on the bad days so you can keep moving forward.

You need faith in yourself to succeed. With confidence, you can go far. Without it, you stay where you are.

*With confidence, you can go far.
Without it, you stay where you are.*

Let's be clear. I'm not talking about egotism ("Me first"), grandiosity ("I am the greatest"), or arrogance ("I'm better than you"). Their roots lie in fear and insecurity. You want none of that.

You want the confidence that says, "This is wonderful! Check it out!" or "I can help you with that" or "Here is what you're looking for."

You want the self-assurance that says, "I am so glad I could help you with that" or "Thank you for letting me serve you today" or "I really appreciate your coming in to check it out."

In short, you want confidence rooted in love. In your heart. In your authentic self.

This book will help you gain that confidence.

How do I know that?

Because confidence is your natural state of being. It's part of who you are. You may have lost sight of it, but it's been inside of you all the time.

This book will help you reconnect with your natural-born confidence by showing you how to honor your mind, heart, body and soul in light and loving ways far beyond bubble baths and manicures—delightful as they are.

And when you honor yourself, you can love your way to success, rather than struggle to get there.

Let me start by asking you:

Why do you want to start (or expand) your dream business?

Think about it for a minute.

If you're not sure why you want to develop your own business, this is a perfect time to think about it. It's hard to build anything significant without a meaningful reason that inspires you to take action. A heartfelt "why" will motivate you more effectively than a hundred pep talks.

You can take a moment now to consider the reasons why you want to create your own business. It could be:

Money – You're tired of struggling to bring in more cash. You want a higher income. Having your own business lets you directly reap the financial rewards for your efforts. None of that commission nonsense, or a stingy salary, or a miserly minimum wage. When you have your own business, you have access to all the money your company makes—maybe even enough to hire staff, or outsource some of your tasks, so you can focus on doing what you do best.

Freedom – You're sick of answering to a boss. You want the freedom to set your own goals, decide on your schedule, set your prices, determine your working hours, and choose where you work. If you need a mental health day—or week, or month—you can take it. If you want to take six months off to explore a place you've always wanted to see, you can go for it.

Fulfillment – You want to give more of yourself and your talents than what your current job asks of you. Or you have a lot to give, but no one wants to hire you to do it. Perhaps you've never heard of a job or a company that does what you want to do. Which means that if you want to make money doing something you love, follow the path you feel guided to take, or do work that reflects your personal values—starting your own business is a great way to go.

Creative Expression – You're a creative, sensitive person who can't or won't play the role your family wants you to play. Let's say your mother wants you to be a professional—a physician, an attorney—so you will always have your own money. Trouble is, you want to design jewelry or write a screenplay or something equally fun but not necessarily high-paying. Turning your creative talents into a thriving business gives you a shot at creating a working life that fulfills you. It might even satisfy your mother.

Or, you've had to fight for the right to express yourself when others wanted you to be quiet and play nice. You've become a warrior for your creativity, and I honor you for that. But perhaps you've grown weary of the struggle. Anger, conflict, and rebellion can be exhausting. Maybe it's time to realize that it's not rage that gives you power. It's a way to connect with your power. The spark of anger works better as ignition than as fuel—it's good to get you started but draining if it's all you use to keep going. You can just as easily connect with your power through love, commitment, or fierce desire—among other things.

This book will help you connect with your power through confidence, so you can start or expand a creativity-based business that's both successful and soul-satisfying.

One caveat: Success cannot be guaranteed. No one can predict the future. But I can promise you that your best, happiest, and most courageous self will emerge as you take inspired action toward your dreams.

You Can Do This

Let me remind you of a few things you may have forgotten about yourself …

You have a **distinctive energy** that only you possess, of all who have ever lived or will ever live on planet Earth. A unique voice. A one-of-a-kind way of seeing the world.

You have **strengths** you're aware of, strengths you are unaware of, and other powers you felt sure you did not have until, one day when you needed them—shazam!—there they were.

You have been given **gifts and talents**, knacks and abilities.

You have **invaluable skills**: some, you were born with; others, you've developed.

You have been given gifts so you can share them. And you are the only one who can give them.

You have been given gifts so you can share them.
And you are the only one who can give them.

You picked up this book because it called out to you. The beckoning of your dream business can feel urgent or inviting. It can sound like a whisper or a shout. It can look liked a faded photograph or a singing, dancing, Technicolor extravaganza.

Whatever it looks like, it's *your* calling. And for reasons that are important to you, you have put off responding to it until now.

I know how the habit of delaying action drains your energy. The heavy burden of something waiting to be done. The disappointment you feel in yourself. Ouch.

I am here to ease the pain of procrastination by helping you make up your mind about whether you want to commit to starting or expanding your dream business.

If you decide "No," you can delete "Develop my dream business" from your to-do list for now, without shame or regret. You can always revisit the idea later if you wish. As long as you're still breathing, it's never too late to start anything.

If you decide "Yes," stay with me to peacefully connect with the confidence you need to succeed—in work and in life.

Why It's Hard to Have Confidence in Yourself

If you have difficulty feeling confident, it's not your fault. Self-confidence will never be a one-and-done decision where you say, "Okay, I have faith in myself. I'm going to get on with my life now."

Confidence is more complicated than that. It's a state of being that reflects your entire consciousness, which occupies several different dimensions at the same time.

For instance, you may beat up on yourself because it feels normal, even necessary, to do so. It can be hard to break the habit of shaming yourself because its roots lie in more than one aspect of your awareness, which includes:

Mind: Thinking hurtful or unsupportive thoughts about yourself and believing that they're true diminishes your self-confidence. Shaming thoughts weaken your ability, even your desire, to believe in yourself.

Heart: If you have a tender heart that bruises easily—and many creative women do—you may feel too insecure to believe in, or connect with, the inner confidence and strength that live inside of you.

Body: Body issues affect your confidence at a profound level. Every hateful thought you think about your appearance grieves your body, which loves you, and makes your heart feel as though a dagger has been plunged into it.

Spirit: Some families believe they have to break a child's spirit to train her, as if she were a puppy instead of a human being. Those who do so may have tried to crush a child's spirit for her own good (as they believed), or so it would be easier to control her, or because their parents did it to them and it's all they know. In any case, the trauma of emotional, verbal, or physical abuse as a child makes it hard to have faith in oneself as an adult.

Genes: Your DNA may carry a predisposition to treat yourself and/or others with anger, contempt, or resentment. It may come from those who raised you (see "Spirit," above) or go back to earlier generations of your family.

Neurology: Cellular memory, neural architecture, and brain chemistry affect the extent to which you can and will have faith in yourself.

Psychology: Many people believe fear, frustration, or rage will motivate you to improve yourself or your circumstances despite decades of studies showing that loving encouragement yields stronger and more consistent motivation than nagging or shaming.

With so many influences in play, it can be challenging to have confidence in yourself on a daily basis. More often, your degree of confidence is as changeable as the weather, depending on circumstances both internal and external.

If you have trouble believing in yourself, you are in good company. Even highly accomplished women wrestle with feelings of not-enoughness.

Michelle Obama, in her best-selling memoir *Becoming*, writes about the feelings of "I'm not good enough" that plagued her even in the White House.

Selena Gomez confessed to *Vogue* that she felt like she wasn't good enough, leading her to cancel parts of a major tour so she could get treatment for anxiety and depression.

Studies show that children raised in alcoholic, abusive, or narcissistic families often grow into adults who feel like they're not good enough, regardless of how much they achieve.

Maybe you feel it, too.

There's nothing wrong with feeling unworthy of the good you desire—a dream business, a wonderful relationship, excellent health, wealth beyond measure, and any other blessings you want.

And there is nothing wrong with you for feeling "I am not enough." There's a lot of it rattling around in the collective consciousness.

Yet you don't have to allow feelings of inadequacy or unworthiness to rule you. You are bigger than your emotions. You are greater than your fears. You are stronger and smarter than you know.

You are stronger and smarter than
you know.

This book will help you build confidence from the inside out, so you have faith that you can handle the ups and downs experienced by every business owner.

If you are willing to be inspired …

If you want to do what you came here to do …

If you would love to express your creativity full-out, loud and proud and prosperous …

You have come to the right place.

This Book is For You If …

You want to leave your job. If you start your own business, you can be your own boss. No more supervisors hovering over you or handing you a big responsibility without the authority to get it done. Plus, you could make more money at your company as a consultant rather than as an employee.

Trouble is, it's hard to walk away from a steady paycheck and benefits. Even though you know the easiest way to segue from a job to your own business is to do your work on the side until the income it brings in matches your paycheck … somehow you can never find the time to get it going.

I get it. You have a big, busy life, like most of us. Who has the time or energy to start something new?

Your job left you, and you're running out of leads on new positions. Starting your own business is beginning to look like a possibility. Maybe even a necessity, if interviews for jobs in your field are few and far between.

With countless companies downsizing, merging, or going under, the era of the 40-year career with one firm is vanishing. The gig economy is replacing it. Maybe it's time to create a gig you love.

My guess: part of you already knows what you would like your gig to be, but you doubt your ability to pull it off. You're facing enough uncertainty as it is. You can't deal with more.

I get it. You're anxious about the future. That's completely understandable, given your situation.

You have a dream, though you may call it something else—a calling, a gift, a goal, an exciting idea that won't leave you alone, a gut feeling that you're meant for bigger and better things—or something else your heart yearns toward.

You want to pursue your dream but have no idea where to start—especially if you've never built a business from scratch before—yet you cannot rest until you start heading in the direction you feel called to go.

I get it. Pursuing a dream, goal, or calling requires a leap of faith, which can feel both scary and exciting.

You have creativity bursting out of your pores—too much to be contained in the narrow confines of a 9-to-5 job. You want to venture out on your own to blaze a unique trail for yourself.

Outside of not knowing where start—and uncertainty about whether you can actually make money doing your thing—you're ready to rock and roll.

I get it. You've probably been told by well-meaning people that creative individuals never make a dime, or that you don't have enough talent to make it big. It's hard to take a chance on yourself if no one believes in you—not even you.

You launched a creative business, and it's floundering. You want to stay with it, but your bills aren't getting paid. You don't know if you can keep your doors open much longer.

You're scared and heartsick. You took a chance on your vision and it's not working out. What will you do if your big dream goes down in flames?

I get it. It's hard to keep faith when things go south. Fear narrows your focus, blinding you to options that might be right in front of you.

You launched a creative business, and it's time to expand. You're excited, but also scared. You never thought your business would get this big. You're feeling overwhelmed.

People want more of you and what you have to offer. How will you meet their demands without ending up even more exhausted than you are right now?

I get it. When you're caught up in the whirl of a successful business, it's hard to slow down. It's even harder to imagine yourself doing more than you are already doing. Naturally, you would love to make the most of the opportunities coming your way—If only you had the energy to act on them.

You're looking for something to give you certainty as you move forward. Many women who want to launch their own business seek out expert advice. Some crave step-by-step blueprints. Others want to make sure they get it right—especially if they have never created a small business before.

I get it. The desire for certainty is understandable. Creating a business from scratch can feel exciting, overwhelming, and terrifying. Naturally, you want some assurance that your investment of time, money and energy will pay off in the form of a booming business.

If you can do several things, which one should you do? It's hard to feel confident that you're making the right choice when you like all your options and don't want to give up any of them. That makes it difficult to get started. You're afraid of choosing the wrong thing, so you do nothing.

If you see only a few possibilities for starting or expanding a business, none of which appeal to you, it's difficult to get excited enough to go forward. What's the point of doing all that work to create something that makes you feel *meh*?

If you're uncertain about what you want, it's challenging to create a business that is right for you. What you want changes from one day to the next. It's like trying to build a house on quicksand.

If any of these situations sound like yours—you have definitely come to the right place. Welcome!

Why Confidence is Hard for Creative Women Entrepreneurs

Many women—including you, perhaps—are taught to put others first. To support the dreams of others while their own dreams die of neglect. To help others get what they want before thinking about what they themselves want. This pattern shows up in different cultures throughout the world and throughout history, so you're not alone.

But as an entrepreneur, your work, by its very nature, invites you to go where no one has gone before. To think differently. To do things in a fresh new way. To shine your light as only you can.

And since you're creating your business from the ground up, or taking it to the next level, you might as well build it the way you want it.

You can give yourself the gift of a business that lets you work the way you want to work, give what you love giving, and receive generous compensation in return.

As a creative female entrepreneur, you are in a league of your own. Forget trying to fit anyone else's idea of what you should be doing. Only you know what is right for you. The business that will be most successful and satisfying for you will be as unique as your thumbprint.

This book will help you get clarity on what is important to you. When you know what matters most to you, you can lovingly build it into your successful, satisfying business.

This book is for women who are excited about launching or expanding their own business and are ready to rock it—if only they knew where to begin.

I wish I could have read this book when my calling came knocking at the door because there's nothing like launching a new business to bring up your emotional issues. Any underlying self-doubt, dread of making a mistake, or fear of rejection will rise up and smack you in the face. Which can really throw you off-balance when you're on the massive learning curve of becoming an entrepreneur.

It's not just you who feels uncertain. You are far from alone, my friend. And I am here for you.

The thing is, your gifts were meant to be shared. That is why they were given to you. The world needs them.

More importantly, *you* need to give your gifts. It's what you were born to do. Who wants to die with their song left unsung?

Fair warning: Some ideas in this book may sound a little woo-woo to you. Whether you're into woo-ville or not, I encourage you to just go with the flow; you will find insight, inspiration, and information you can use, whatever you believe or don't believe.

This book will help you serenely set aside your doubts and gain the confidence you need to share your unique gifts as a business, rather than as a hobby you do in your spare time.

It positions you to joyfully build a prosperous, richly fulfilling life by doing something you enjoy … one confident step at a time.

What Will You Feel Like After Reading This Book?

You will gain a new appreciation for all the gifts you bring to your business, to your life, and to the world—a great confidence-booster.

You will feel more trust in yourself, your instincts, and your abilities.

You may even let go of looking outside yourself for answers. For permission. For validation. Because you know, deep in your bones, that you can follow your heart with confidence and joy.

You are enough, and more than enough, exactly as you are. This book will help you see that more clearly than ever, so you can get on with doing what you came here to do with a loving heart and a peaceful mind.

Let's get started, shall we?

Master Your Mind

"The chief enemy of creativity is good sense."

—Pablo Picasso

Your creative gifts and talents are needed. It's great that you're willing to share them in a way that profits you as well as others. That way, everyone wins. How exciting is that?

Since it's your company, you can build it up any way you want. You can bring forth a business the world has never seen before, using the feelings and colors, thoughts and words, that pour through your imagination and into the world we live in.

The possibilities are endless.

Here's the thing: limitless possibilities can be confusing. If you have the power to create anything at all, it can be hard to decide what to do first. And next. And after that.

When you have many options to choose from, it can create decision fatigue and analysis paralysis, to the point where you end up doing nothing rather than risk making the wrong move.

And that would be a pity, because the world needs your gifts now more than ever. And you need to give them.

Play around for a moment with ideas about the business you would like to build or expand. Pretend you're free to create your company whatever way you want. Forget about what pundits and experts and your father-in-law tell you about starting a business. Focus on the way you want to do it.

Your business, if you want it to be both satisfying and successful, must reflect you: your unique personality, creativity, soul, and values. So, you get to decide how it's going to look and feel.

If you're like many creative women, you may have lost track of who you truly are or what you really want. Our families, our culture, our society, and even the collective consciousness often discourage women from freely expressing themselves. As a result, we shut ourselves down. We go along to get along. In doing so, we forget our true selves.

It happens.

Going along to get along is a widespread survival strategy. There is nothing wrong with you for having bowed to familial or societal pressures. It's normal. Your brain has been hard-wired through millions of years of evolution to collaborate and cooperate with others for the good of the tribe.

However, as a creative woman, you're already an outlier. You may have grown up wondering how on Earth you ended up with the family you have. Your family may have wondered the same thing, branding you as the black sheep (or white sheep, or pink sheep) of the clan.

You may be one of the fortunate women who grew up with people who celebrate creativity and honor individuality.

If that's you—congratulations! You're starting your business miles ahead of those who have spent their lives walking the tightrope between being true to themselves and pleasing their loved ones.

Whatever your situation, this book will help you gain clarity about who you are and what you want, so you can build satisfaction as well as success into your small business.

By coming to a deeper understanding of what success means to you personally, you increase the odds that your business will succeed. Meaning that it will nourish and support you financially, physically, mentally, emotionally, spiritually, and creatively.

In this book, we will explore the Five Confidence Keys that will support you in creating or growing a successful, satisfying business.

Let's begin with the first Confidence Key: Master Your Mind.

Why Mastering Your Mind Matters in Your Business

Your mind has extraordinary powers.

It can fill you with joy or plunge you into despair.

It can set you free to explore the wide world or imprison you in a cage that exists only between your ears.

It can inspire you to lovingly reach out to others or make you withdraw into yourself, leaving you feeling alone and afraid.

In the context of your creative business, your mind can take you out of the game faster than you can say, "There's no way I can make money doing this."

A statement like this is more than a thought. It is a decision. You have made up your mind—so far, at least—that there is no way you can make money doing something you love.

And, as Henry Ford pointed out, "Whether you think you can or whether you think you can't—you're right."

Neuroscientists explain this truism as the *confirmation bias*. It means your brain invites experiences that confirm your beliefs to come into your awareness and dismisses or explains away experiences that contradict your beliefs.

For instance, your brain, following your "no way to make money doing this" directive, will make every effort to prove you're right—there *is* no way to make money doing something you love—such as:

It will talk you out of saying "Yes" to lucrative opportunities.

Drive you to spend a fortune on workshops and then discourage you from applying your new skills to your business.

Mute your creative muse.

Make you say the wrong thing at the wrong moment to your best client.

Distract you from doing your work by insisting, "I've got to vacuum first" or "It would be better to wait until after the holiday to do this."

Your brain can stop your business in its tracks—all for the sake of confirming that you are correct in believing that you can't make money doing something you love.

Your mind does this because it loves you.

I know. It's a weird way to show love, but there it is.

Let's see why that happens, so we can change it.

Three Ways Your Brain Can Stop You and Your Business

Being "Realistic"

One of the most common ways I've seen smart, creative women shoot down their business—sometimes even before they launch it—is by being "realistic."

Nine times out of ten, their so-called realistic thoughts are actually negative thoughts. These ideas come dressed up as good sense, practicality, "let's get real here," and other disguises that convince you it would be foolish to ignore them.

That's what makes being realistic so insidious. It sounds too reasonable to argue with. It *makes sense.*

Your brain loves it when things make sense. It figures that if you can understand the world and the way it works, you will be safe. And that is what it wants. Your brain wants you to be safe because it loves you.

Ironically, what most people call realistic thinking is highly unrealistic. Negative thinking has nothing to do with reality, which is what is happening here and now.

Negative thinking can be thought of as an aspect of your brain's confirmation bias: it hides any evidence that contradicts your beliefs and judgments so you can keep believing what you want to believe.

For example, if something did not work before, negative thinking says it will not work now. It makes sense, as far as it goes. But all it shows us is the limits of logic. Even if something failed five times in the past, that has nothing to do with whether it can work today.

That's because this is a new day. Things have changed. The universe has expanded. Technology has advanced. People are different. Most importantly, you are smarter today than you were yesterday.

Even if you previously tried and failed to launch your company, for example, that was then. This is now. Anything can happen, and that is good news for you, my friend. *Anything* can happen, including a successful business that satisfies your soul.

Anything *can happen, including a successful business that satisfies your soul.*

Demolishing Your Confidence

From an evolutionary standpoint, your brain thinks self-confidence is a terrible idea. It figures that if you have faith in yourself, you will go out and do something dangerous and die.

One of its ways of protecting you from overconfidence involves something neuroscientists call the *negativity bias*: the mind's tendency to retain painful memories and erase positive memories. This explains why hurtful experiences haunt us long after they're over, while we struggle to remember good times that happened more than five minutes ago.

Let's watch the negativity bias at work.

Say you've done a few interior design projects for friends and they've been encouraging you to go professional. Because you're smart enough to create your business the way you want it right from the start, you make a list of the kind of projects you want to specialize in. You especially delight in bringing beauty to residential living rooms and patios, so these will be the first services you offer as a professional interior decorator.

Your mind, seeing that confidence is leading you into danger (a.k.a. the unknown), leaps into action. It thunders into your inner ear, "Remember that time you painted Sally's living room the wrong shade of white? It should have been Navaho White, and you used Chantilly Lace! You have no eye for color at all! There is no way you can succeed in this business!"

If you fold up under this shaming onslaught—and many people would— that is the end of your business right there. In the future, if you think about starting your business, the ghost of Navaho White (or other bloopers) will rise up to remind you that you are not good enough to turn professional.

Thanks to your ever-loving brain, countless people whose houses you could have beautified, whose eyes you could have enchanted with harmonizing colors, whose spirits could have been healed by the sanctuary you created for them, will miss out on the unique vision of home that only you could have provided.

Limiting Your Point of View

When you were an infant, your mind developed the habit of *generalizing,* to make sense of the approximately eleven million bits of information entering your brain every second of every day.

This mental organizing system works well in terms of identifying and sorting objects, like recognizing that a bench, a bar stool, and a rocking chair are all things you can sit on.

Where many of us get into trouble is in using generalizations to help us figure out life and relationships.

It begins when you're a child. Your brain figures that the way it is at home is the way it is everywhere. The way your loved ones treat you is the way people are supposed to treat each other. And people who do things differently must be wrong, or bad, or special in a way that you will never be special.

The brain's generalizations can work against you, as well as others.

Let's see how childhood generalizations can affect your feelings about money.

If you grew up in a wealthy family, it can set you up to create a successful and satisfying business because you're accustomed to the best of everything.

On the other hand, if your parents lavished you with money instead of the affection you craved, you may despise money in general. This makes it hard to show a profit in your business because money stays away from people who don't like it.

Alternatively, you may be accustomed to other people doing the hard work, while you passively receive the cash they generate. This can lead to the disempowering assumption that other people can make money, but not you. It also can produce an attitude of entitlement that rubs clients, colleagues, investors, and vendors the wrong way.

I have also worked with women who resented their wealth because they could never be sure whether people liked them for themselves. A feeling of resentment toward money tends to make it avoid you, which can spell disaster for your business.

Also, some women who grew up rich felt guilty about having lots of money when others have so much less. To correct this perceived unfairness, they give away or throw away large amounts of money. Divesting oneself of riches may salve the conscience, but you will rapidly go broke if you do the same in your business.

If you grew up in a lower- or middle-class family, it can set you up to generate massive success in your business because you have a solid work ethic.

On the other hand, if you or your family resented the more well-off families in the neighborhood, you may have grown up convinced that money makes you greedy, snobbish, or selfish. This makes it hard to allow yourself to be successful, because you're worried that fame or fortune will turn you into a bad person.

Alternatively, you may imagine that no matter how hard you work, you will never rise above the income level you grew up with. This can become a self-fulfilling prophecy.

Part of you may even believe it would be wrong for you to make more money than your mother or father—that they would feel hurt, shamed, or betrayed. No loving daughter wants to hurt a parent like that. She would rather have her business go down in flames than wound her loved ones.

If you grew up broke, it can serve as a powerful motivator to lift yourself up by creating a hugely successful and satisfying business.

On the other hand, if you or your family took pride in your ability to scrape by and survive despite tremendous odds, just getting by can become a way of life. When things get too easy, you wonder when the trouble will start. When you're having a good time, you wait for the calamity that will surely follow. These, too, can become self-fulfilling prophecies that will sink your business.

Alternatively, if you grew up poor, you may have a hard time imagining anything better for yourself than what you had, or now have. It's like your brain has gotten hooked on the chemicals of hopelessness and it regards anyone who offers you hope or help with grave suspicion: What do they want from you? Are they trying to take advantage of you? It's hard to attract top-notch assistants, colleagues, and partners when you have a mistrustful attitude. They won't have it. They know they deserve better.

I have also worked with women at all income levels who have a profound sense of bitterness or helplessness when it comes to money. They hate having to think about it. They wish they could avoid dealing with money altogether.

Some women who make a lower income wish they could win the lottery; a reflection of their belief that they are powerless to generate a large income on their own.

Some who are more well-off feel sad and isolated because, despite their wealth, they still have problems. Where can they turn, when money hasn't provided the solutions it seemed to promise? Every day, headlines scream the news about rich, unhappy people headed for rehab, the divorce court, jail, or worse.

The bottom line: If you want to build a successful and satisfying business, it's essential to make peace with money. Otherwise your business will end up as a hobby that eats cash rather than makes it.

The first step: recognize that money carries a neutral energy. It is neither good nor bad. It just *is*, like water and air.

Money can never make you a good person or a bad person. It simply makes you more of who you are. It gives your creativity more room to play, which can only enrich your business while satisfying your soul.

Three Ways to Train Your Brain to Build a Successful Business

The wacky ways your brain ensures your safety—confirmation bias, negativity bias, and generalizing—began as survival strategies.

Millions of years of evolution hard-wired these tendencies into your brain. They haven't outlived their usefulness. It's just that they've taken over the shop. Your brain is working overtime to protect you from imagined dangers as well as genuine threats to your safety.

While you can't stop your mind from spewing out negative notions that keep you playing small, you can change the way you relate to your thoughts.

The thoughts you think—however weird or wonderful they may be—matter far less than the way you respond to them.

Here are some sane and compassionate ways to transform your relationship with your mind, so you can team up to build a satisfying and successful business—as well as a life rich in joy and meaning.

Stop Believing Everything You Think

When you're excited about a new project, person, or opportunity, the last thing you want to hear is someone saying, "Do you really think it's going to work out? Get over yourself!"

And yet, you may talk to yourself like that. You may even pull the plug on your thrilling new creative venture to avoid the possibility of disappointment.

If you want to stop wrecking golden opportunities with self-sabotaging thoughts, it's essential to realize that you are not your thoughts. You are a person who *has* thoughts.

You are not your thoughts.
You are a person who has *thoughts.*

That's why beating up on yourself for thinking negative thoughts makes no sense. Those ideas show up without any help from you, so they are not your fault. They're just your brain talking to itself.

You can't choose your thoughts, because you didn't make them. But you can choose to respond to them in a different way.

If your mind says something unsupportive, like "This didn't work out the last time I tried it," you can respond with, "Yes, and that was then. This is now."

Or, you can call up memories of times when things worked out well, to remind your brain that good stuff happens for you, too.

Or you can simply choose a different thought. Preferably a compassionate and supportive thought, so you can build the confidence and courage to launch or expand your business.

Your brain makes up everything you think. Therefore, an encouraging thought is just as true—and just as false—as a discouraging thought.

So, you might as well place your focus on uplifting thoughts and beliefs as you build your business. Try it out. See what happens.

Treating your thoughts with kind attention is a new habit. Give it some time. Be patient and compassionate with yourself as you cultivate this fresh way of thinking about your thoughts.

Stop Complaining

It can be such a relief to complain. You feel better after you've griped about the stuff that makes you unhappy. You feel justified in your misery.

Why would I ask you to stop grousing?

It's because complaining fools your brain into thinking you have taken action to remedy the state of affairs you've been moaning about.

You see, venting with your friends releases some of the stress and strain you've been feeling. When the burden lifts, your brain figures, "I must have fixed that problem, because I feel better now." And so, you do nothing to change the situation you're suffering through.

This makes sense, as far as it goes: "I kvetched + I feel better now = The problem is solved." It's rational, in an irrational sort of way.

Trouble is, the mess is still there. Every time you complain about it, you cement the situation more firmly into your reality because you keep thinking about it. And what you focus on expands. The more you think and talk about the problem, the bigger it gets.

As a bonus, grumbling drains away your motivation to make a positive change. Your brain has concluded that the complaints have solved the problem. Further action appears unnecessary.

Look, nobody here wants you to turn into a positive-thinking Pollyanna. That mentality has its own pitfalls, like denying your pain, which is an act of profound self-abandonment.

Another option: stop thinking about your problem. Just for a minute.

Temporarily set aside your judgments against the situation ("It sucks"), other people involved ("She's a b----"), and yourself ("I'm so stupid to have gotten into this mess").

Instead, focus on the way the situation makes you feel. Be honest with yourself about your emotions. If you're living or working in toxic circumstances, you have every right to feel the way you feel. In fact, it would be kind of weird if you liked feeling miserable.

Let yourself feel your feelings instead of talking about them. If you're sad, allow yourself to cry or wail. If you're angry or frustrated, stamp your feet. If you're anxious, shake it out.

In short, do something physical to express your feelings. This way, your body can release your pent-up emotional energy instead of letting it build up until you explode, which often makes a bad situation worse.

Do your emotional releasing in private. You will feel freer to fully express your true feelings if nobody is watching.

It's amazing how your mind clears once you've allowed yourself to feel and release your emotions. New ideas about how to resolve the matter can rise up in your mind. Hidden blessings in the situation may reveal themselves to you. The way forward can become clear.

Some people call complaining "keeping it real." Well, it's even more real to face your situation with the intention to resolve it in a way that honors all concerned. Starting with you.

In a business context, it's worth remembering that complainers tend to see themselves as the walking wounded.

Very few people want to do business with a victim, unless they are wounded, too. Victims tend to find one another because the energy of emotional pain feels like home to them. Shared suffering may create strong bonds, but it will never empower you or your clients.

Also, con artists smell out folks who reek of victimhood because they make easy prey. I suggest you avoid being on your guard against predators, since guardedness walls you off from love, money, and creativity as well as danger. Instead, be mindful. Alertness works far better than fear when it comes to protecting you and your business.

Alertness works far better than fear when it comes to protecting you and your business.

In short, you'll attract a better class of client if you stop letting complaints dominate your conversations.

Ask for Right Perception

The *Course in Miracles* teaches that the only miracle we ever need to pray for is the miracle of right perception.

Or, as Wayne Dyer put it, "When you change the way you look at things, the things you look at change."

For instance, let's say your business hasn't been bringing in enough money. Too little income can be scary. It can also foster self-doubt: "Maybe I'm not good enough. If I were better at what I do, I'd be making more money."

So, you're looking at your bank balance and seeing disaster. Maybe you're also feeling ashamed, frustrated, or disappointed. Good times.

You can use this moment to take a deep breath or two. Quiet your mind.

Make a connection with your Higher Power and say, "Help me to see this situation in a new light. Give me right perception of what's going on here."

Sit quietly for a few minutes. Notice what comes to mind.

You may suddenly remember your last networking meeting, where a real estate agent expressed interest in your work. You never followed up with her. Maybe this is a good time to get in touch to see if you can be of service to her and her colleagues.

Or, your website's home page may appear in your mind's eye and you think, "That home page hasn't been updated in years. Maybe I should look it over and see if it speaks to the people I want to serve. Maybe I've lost touch with my audience and their needs."

Whatever way you experience right perception, you can trust it if it is compassionate and free of blame toward you or anyone else. If it involves shaming or blaming, it's not right perception. Most likely, your ego-mind crashed the party. Get quiet again and keep asking for right perception until you get supportive guidance. It's there for you at any time.

The practice of asking for right perception can serve you in all areas of your life.

It helps you see your loved ones more clearly.

It helps you see yourself more compassionately.

It can lift you up when you feel low.

It can guide you toward new and satisfying ways to create and conduct your business.

It can show you how to work well with those you came here to serve, in ways that profit you as well as those you help.

Right perception is always there for the asking. You just need to remember to ask.

How Laura Got Her Dream Job

Laura came to me to figure out the best way to do her two businesses: interior decoration using Feng Shui and art direction for television shows.

"I'm not getting much business, either with homes or with TV work," Laura said. "It's frustrating. I work so hard, but I'm barely making ends meet."

"Of course, you're frustrated," I said. "Anyone would be when you put so much of yourself into your work and get so little in return. Let's see what's going on under the surface here."

I tuned in to Higher Consciousness and said, "The first thing I'm getting is that you're worn out from splitting your focus. It tires your brain to keep switching gears between working in homes and working on sets."

"It's true," Laura confirmed. "I didn't mention it before, but I'm exhausted all the time."

"I'll bet you are. How would you feel about concentrating on just one business for now?"

"I don't know. I guess I could. It's just that I don't really like doing the home décor, even though it's easier to get jobs doing houses than TV shows.

"I don't want to give up on my dream of working in television, but I don't think I can get enough projects to keep me going." She sighed. "There are so many good people out there. Too many. How will I ever get enough work to make a living?"

"I don't know," I said. "Tell me this. Which of these two businesses do you love most?"

"Oh! The TV work, hands down. I love the people, the fast pace on set, the challenge of making something beautiful on time and on budget … I wish I could do it all the time!"

"Fair enough. Would it be all right if your Higher Power showed you why you are worthy and ready to get steady work in television?"

She gasped, "Yes!"

"Would it be okay if your Higher Power shows you why it's safe for you to focus your attention on the TV work, and what will happen if you do?"

"Oh, my gosh! Yes!" Laura's eyes were shining.

We worked along these lines for the rest of our session. Laura hugged me before she left. "I feel amazing! Thank you! And I feel like something amazing is going to happen!"

She called me an hour later.

"You're not going to believe what just happened!" Laura said. "I've got a job decorating the set for my favorite comedienne's talk show!"

"Wow, that was fast! Tell me about it."

"She just called me out of the blue and offered me the job. I hadn't applied for it—I didn't even know there was an opening!

"She said she's been frustrated with her current set decorator for a while, and today she decided she was going to replace her. She asked herself, 'Out of all the set decorators I know, who would I really love to work with?' My name came to mind … and she called to offer me the job.

"It's perfect! I love working with her … the studio is less than 15 minutes from my house … and the job is full time with full benefits! I start work in two weeks!" She took a breath. "It's like a miracle!"

By now, we were both tearing up with joy and gratitude.

"I'm so happy for you, Laura! That is the best news ever—and you totally deserve it! You'll do a fantastic job!"

"I don't know how to thank you. You're incredible!"

I smiled. "We're both incredible. Let me know how it goes, okay?"

It worked out even better than expected. Laura's work thrilled the talk show host. She won the hearts of her crew as they produced first-class work under her direction.

Laura remained with the talk show until it was canceled two years later. More work came her way as soon as she was available.

Three years after our session, Laura won an Emmy Award for set decoration.

You Can Do It, Too

Laura had a story going on in her mind that she wasn't good enough to do the work she loved.

She also believed it would be hard to find work in television, so she would have to continue doing interior design if she wanted to make a living.

These beliefs became self-fulfilling prophecies.

When we looked at Laura's stories about why she couldn't have what she wanted through the eyes of right perception, the limiting beliefs that kept her struggling fell away.

Once Laura changed her mind, her circumstances changed, too.

The point is, the mind has great power.

Your mind has great power.

You can use it to go toward your dreams or deny them.

You can use it to light your way or keep you in the dark.

You get to decide where you want to direct your mind's creative powers.

Take a moment to think about a dream you would like to set in motion today.

If you had infinite choices before you, what would you choose?

Before you strain your brain trying to figure out which option you want, remember this:

It's only your mind that says you have to choose between chocolate or vanilla, love or money, success or fulfillment.

The Universe is bigger than that.

As you gain right perception, you will begin to see that more options are available to you than you ever imagined.

Join me in the next chapter to find out more.

Honor Your Heart

"Once we believe in ourselves, we can risk curiosity, wonder, spontaneous delight or any experience that reveals the human spirit."

—e e cummings

If you're a creative woman, emotions play a big role in your life and in your work.

When joy zings through you, you feel unstoppable. You walk with a spring in your step. You do your creative work with zest. You smile at strangers walking by. You're kind to your loved ones and kind to yourself. And that makes you feel even better.

The bottom line: Setting up and running your business feels wonderful when you feel good about yourself and your work.

On the other hand, if negative feelings grab you by the throat, you can hardly catch your breath. Whether you're seized by panic, anger, fear, frustration, or some other gut-wrenching emotion—your brain seems to shut down. It's hard to think straight. It's harder to be productive. And it's nearly impossible to feel good about anything you produce under these conditions because it carries the negative vibe you felt when you created it.

The bottom line: Setting up and running your business feels like a back-breaking burden when you're swept up in a tsunami of painful emotions.

I'm not suggesting that you shut down or ignore your negative emotions and think shiny, pretty thoughts all the time. That is not only impossible, it's inhuman. Feelings will not be denied. They will only get stronger until you give them the attention they call for.

Instead, consider learning how to handle yourself and your feelings with love, respect, and understanding.

Why Honoring Your Feelings Matters in Your Business

When you can acknowledge your feelings without letting them run the show, you greatly increase your chances of creating a business—and a life—that is successful and satisfying.

If you live in the center of an emotional hurricane, you're not going to get very far.

And I'd like to see you get as far as you want to go. You deserve it.

Why It's Hard to Handle Your Feelings

If you have no idea how to handle your feelings—if you didn't even know it was possible to handle your feelings—it's not your fault.

Chances are, you grew up with emotionally illiterate people who passed their cluelessness on to you. It's not their fault, either. They could only teach you what they knew. No one is to blame.

In any case, you had no one to show you how to treat yourself, your feelings, and other people with respect.

Emotional illiteracy comes in many flavors, including:

Feelings Mean You're Weak

In some families and cultures, showing your feelings is considered a sign of weakness. You're taught to hide your emotions to help you avoid losing face, revealing vulnerability, or leaving yourself open to attack.

In these circumstances, it's often considered best to have no feelings at all. This leaves you unprepared to deal with your emotions in any sane or compassionate way.

Shutting down is a common way of dealing with unruly emotions. But when you cut yourself off from your feelings, you cut yourself off from others ... from love ... even from yourself. You and your business will prosper more if you allow yourself to reconnect with your feelings, which are the energy of life itself.

Feelings Must Be Broadcast

In some families and cultures, emotions run rampant. If a person feels a certain way, everyone is going to hear about it, whether they want to or not.

If you are a sensitive and creative person raised in such circumstances, you may have coped by letting your emotions run wild, too, so you could be heard. Or, you may have retreated to your room or the home of a sympathetic friend, because all that drama drained your energy.

In any case, you had no opportunity to learn how to handle your emotions and the emotions of others. These are key skills in life as well as in business.

Feelings Should Be Shared

In some families and cultures, you may be encouraged or even pressured to share your thoughts and feelings—which you may or may not have wanted to do.

As a creative, sensitive person, you may prefer privacy over letting it all hang out. Especially if your loved ones criticize you when you share what's going on with you. It sets the stage for a lifelong habit of beating up on yourself unless you think, feel, and act the "right" way.

When you grow up with folks who frequently put you in the wrong, it's difficult even when you're an adult to feel like anything you do is right. This self-doubt undercuts the confidence every entrepreneur needs to gain the trust of potential clients, customers and investors.

Only One Person's Feelings Matter

Some family circles revolve around one person whose needs must be met at all costs. It may be because they are considered the strongest or the weakest, the healthiest or the sickest, the most talented or the least talented, the most sensitive or the most insensitive, the smartest or the silliest, or simply because they are male and you are female.

If you grew up as the star of the family, you may enter adult life with full confidence that success and approval will meet you everywhere you go. You may have few inner resources to deal with the normal setbacks of life and business. You may also have little empathy for other people, which, in a business context, can lead to a certain tone-deafness in your dealings with clients, customers, colleagues, or investors that will alienate them.

If you grew up in the shadow of your family's star, you may enter adult life feeling like you don't matter, that your creative gifts are worthless, that good things happen for other people but not for you. You may even unconsciously hold yourself back because part of you believes it would be wrong for you to be more successful than the family's star. Low self-worth, in a business context, tends to generate self-sabotaging behaviors like procrastination, overwork, and charging too little for your time, goods, or services. Any one of these behaviors can take down your business.

How to Build Honoring Your Heart into Your Business

If you're like most people with a small business, you give it your all, so it's essential to practice emotional self-care to avoid burnout.

Here are some ways you can honor yourself and your feelings.

Treat Yourself With Compassion

If you make a mistake, cut yourself some slack. In both life and business, you will make mistakes. And it's okay. If you're not making mistakes, you're not trying.

It's much more conducive to peace and productivity if you focus on learning from your error rather than beating yourself up for it. Hint: the lesson is almost never "I'm an idiot" (blaming yourself) or "He betrayed me" (blaming someone else). A true lesson is usually more along the lines of, "I knew that person couldn't be trusted, but I went ahead with our deal anyway. Next time, I'll follow my instincts."

Choose Your Clients With Discernment

When you know you will be spending time with an emotionally demanding or draining client, schedule time to recharge before your next meeting. Take a walk. Read an article in a magazine. Do deep breathing. Whatever it takes, do something to reconnect with your life force both before and after meetings with high-maintenance people.

Also, take time to consider whether the money you make from working with demanding clients is worth the price you pay for doing it. If working with certain people saps your energy, undermines your confidence, or puts you through an emotional meat-grinder—as a business owner, you can't afford to keep them as clients. They cost you too much.

If you sense at your first meeting with a potential client that she is an energy vampire … and she wants to work with you … you can thank her and say you prefer to refer her to another person in your field who you think would be a better fit for her. Then make that referral.

Stop Waiting for Permission to Launch Your Business

Give yourself permission to launch your business. Let go of your insistence on gaining the approval of certain hard-to-please people before you start. Your life belongs to you, and your dreams are just as important as anyone else's.

Just because you haven't started a business before doesn't mean you can't do it. Approach the adventure of launching your own company with a beginner's mind. You have much to learn, and you can learn it. I have faith in you. You are stronger, smarter, and more resourceful than you know.

You are stronger, smarter, and more
resourceful than you know.

Allow Yourself to Be Successful

Give yourself permission to be successful. Step away from the all-too-common tendency to hold yourself back because you're worried that someone you care about will feel bad about themselves if you are successful.

It's sweet of you to care about your loved one's feelings, but you have no control over their emotions. Nothing you do or refrain from doing will make them feel better about themselves. Developing self-esteem is an inside job. You cannot do it for your loved one, however much you may want to. Your loved one will feel the way she feels, regardless of what you do. So, you might as well be successful.

Charge What You and Your Offerings Are Worth

Maybe you have trouble with the idea of asking for payment. You need to get okay with that because your business will go under if your rates are too low to cover your costs and show a profit. It's easier to charge an appropriate price for goods and services when you recognize the value of what you offer.

Your fee or mark-up has nothing to do your personal worth. It reflects the value of what you provide for your clients or customers. When you're setting your fees, the question to ask yourself is "How much value does my work bring to a person's life?" The answer is often "Huge," so charge accordingly.

Make Peace With Marketing

As a business owner, you need to promote your goods or services. If the idea of sales and marketing makes you feel nauseous, you're in good company. A lot of creative women feel the same way.

Forget about trying to make anyone buy from you. People who need convincing are not your people. Direct your offers to folks who want what you're selling. They will find their way to you. It will happen faster—and you will make a profit sooner—if you let people know what you're up to. You do that by marketing your offerings.

Sales and marketing help you serve your clients by making them aware of something that will make their lives better in some way.

Since you're a creative woman, I'll bet you can dream up fun and easy ways to promote your offerings, if you think about it for a few minutes. Let your imagination run wild.

Conduct Yourself With Integrity

It's essential to keep your word with folks you do business with. Your word is your bond as a business owner. If you lack integrity, word will get around and your company will go under.

Here's the thing: sometimes it's impossible to keep an agreement. If you get sick, you may be unable to meet the deadline you agreed on. If you're running behind, you may miss an important appointment. If you and a business partner made an agreement but it's not working out, unspoken resentment will poison your partnership.

The good news: you can retain your integrity if you notify the people involved, in a timely way, that you can't keep the original agreement.

Keep your explanation brief. Suggest negotiating a new agreement that takes the altered circumstances into account. Do what you can to make it right. Work it out—or recognize that it isn't going to work out. Either way, you can learn a valuable lesson from the experience and move on.

How Elise Moved Past Her Fears

Elise had been a stay-at-home mother for several years when she came to me because she wanted to start her own business as an intuitive healer.

She knew she had phenomenal psychic abilities, so she felt well-equipped for the work in that respect.

"But I want to offer more than just reading a person's aura," Elise told me. "I want to help my clients heal. My guidance told me to come to you to train as a healer."

Of course, I felt honored that, of all the instructors in the world, her guides recommended me.

It was a good sign that Elise had enough faith in her guidance to follow it. Trusting your own knowing is vital for any creative person if you want to be effective in the world, in your life, and in your business.

On our first day, we spent a few minutes chatting over coffee before moving on to her training. When it came time to start, Elise suddenly, literally, could not move. Understandably, she got scared.

"My legs won't move! I can't lift up my feet!" Her face contorted with effort as she tried to walk, but her limbs weren't cooperating.

"What's going on?" Elise cried. "Have I had a stroke? Why can't I move?"

"Let me tune in and see what's going on with you," I suggested.

"Okay."

"Here's what I'm getting," I said. "Part of you is terrified of taking this training. Why would that be?"

Elise got quiet. "You're right. Part of me is afraid my life will change forever if I do this training. And part of me feels completely unworthy of doing this work. I'm afraid of failing and disappointing my family. I'm … I'm afraid I'll disappoint God." Tears streamed down her face.

"I understand. It's okay to feel scared," I assured her. "You've taken a huge leap of faith, coming all the way from Austria to do this training. Feeling frightened about it is totally normal. Would you like to understand why it is safe for you to do this training now?"

"Yes," she whispered.

"Good," I said. "Breathe with me."

As we took deep breaths together, I affirmed that Elise now has the highest understanding of why it is safe for her and safe for others—especially her two daughters—for her to take this training now. I also declared that she now clearly sees why she is worthy and ready to do this work.

Within minutes, Elise tried to lift her right foot. It easily came up off the floor. She walked toward me and enveloped me in an affectionate hug.

"Thank you," she said. "Let's get started!"

After our training, Elise went home to Vienna and set up her intuitive healing business. She did well from Day One, because she was—and is—immensely gifted, as well as warm and caring. No wonder people flock to her.

I am so proud of Elise for facing her emotional fears so she could step into her greatness.

You Can Do It, Too

In this story, you saw how Elise's emotions made her body shut down. She physically could not move forward with her training until her fears were addressed. When her feelings healed, her legs regained the ability to walk.

Strong emotions like fear or anger can make your mind shut down, too, making it impossible to think clearly or to make wise choices, as you build your business.

For instance, it's easy to shut yourself down by telling yourself,

"I don't want to be a starving artist."

"Everyone says I'll never make money doing this."

"Intuitive, airy-fairy stuff isn't real work. There's no way I can charge people for it."

"I'm not smart enough to run a business all by myself."

"There's no way I can leave my job. I have to have a regular paycheck."

What are you telling yourself? Would you talk to your worst enemy like that?

If you consistently discourage or demean yourself, it's no wonder you feel defeated before you start. Your emotions tend to follow your mind's lead. If you habitually latch on to wounding thoughts, you will feel too weak to start or expand your dream business.

Unaddressed emotional issues can also drive you to unconscious acts of self-sabotage like procrastination or overwhelm; they make every day a struggle, both personally and professionally.

The answer is not to ignore, overcome, or repress painful emotions. Coping methods like these only drive your feelings underground, where they stew and sour and gain even more power over you.

Your emotions need to be acknowledged and honored. Once you've given them the attention they crave, they usually pass harmlessly through your body and out of your life.

Yes, it takes courage to admit you're scared or angry.

*Your emotions need to be acknowledged
and honored.*

And it takes guts to be willing to see yourself and your fears in a new light. A light that helps you see your magnificence more clearly. A light that lovingly guides you toward the life you were born to live.

Everyone has access to that light—including you, right now, exactly as you are.

You are bigger than your feelings. You are greater than your fears. More powerful than your anger.

Greatness lives within you. It has been here all the time, waiting to be tapped into and expressed. You have everything you need to succeed in your business inside of you right now.

You've got this.

If you have trouble believing that, I get it. You probably made up your mind a long time ago about yourself and what you're capable of achieving.

You are much more than you ever imagined. Maybe it's time to catch up with the truth of who you really are and what is possible for you.

You are more beautiful, strong, and wise than you realize. If you think that's pure hogwash, be sure to check out the next chapter.

Respect Your Body

I believe that the greatest gift you can give your family and the world is a healthy you.

—Joyce Meyers

Years ago, I walked into the locker room at my gym in Hollywood and saw, as usual, about a dozen women in various stages of undress.

One woman had gleaming skin of darkest ebony—a striking contrast to the white blazer and trousers she was putting on.

A pale woman sat facing away from me, revealing a wildly colorful tattoo of a spread eagle that covered her back from neck to hips.

At a mirror, a young Asian woman carefully applied winged eyeliner, emphasizing the sexy slant of her almond eyes.

Next to her at the mirror, a brunette woman in her thirties with rich olive skin used a magnifying glass to peer at her microscopic pores.

All this beauty, in so many different shapes and sizes, surrounded me.

The thought suddenly came to me, "I wonder if any of these women have any idea how beautiful they are?"

My heart felt the answer come back swiftly: "No. And neither do you."

It was true. I never felt beautiful. Passable, perhaps, on a good day, but that was as good as it got. Most days, I avoided looking in the mirror because all I ever saw was pimples and pudge. Occasionally, someone would tell me I was pretty, but I never believed them. Instead, I assumed they wanted something from me.

Through my training and practice in healing, I've discovered a few reasons why I focused on what I considered my body's bad points, while its good points remained invisible to me.

If you, too, have trouble seeing how beautiful you are, this chapter is for you.

Why It's Hard to See Your Own Beauty

Stunning celebrities from Ingrid Bergman and Audrey Hepburn to Rihanna and Penelope Cruz have confessed, "I never *felt* pretty."

Such statements may lead folks to conclude that these beauties must be blind, deluded, or indulging in false modesty for dubious reasons. Yet it's likely these lovelies spoke the truth: regardless of their appearance, they didn't like what they saw in the mirror.

What's up with that?

Reason #1 Why it's Hard to See Your Own Beauty

You are not the best judge of your own appearance

You live inside your skin, with emotions and thoughts and memories that influence the way you perceive your face and body. When you're in a good mood, you're more inclined to like the way you look—hence the cliché, "When you feel good, you look good." If you feel angry or hurt or scared, those feelings can color the way you see your body.

By contrast, the rest of us live outside your skin, so we find it easier to recognize your loveliness.

Reason #2 Why it's Hard to See Your Own Beauty

The opinions of others influence the way you see yourself

If your looks fail to fit the standard of beauty held by your community, you could be considered an ugly duckling when, to other people, you are a swan of unsurpassed beauty.

Your brain is hard-wired to fit in with the people around you, for the sake of survival. So, it would be understandable that if your family thinks you're lacking in the looks department, you would agree with them, even if it made you feel sad or less than.

Another possibility: if your parents think you're gorgeous they may refrain from praising your appearance to keep you from becoming conceited or vain. A girl could live her whole life never knowing her mother and father thought she was beautiful because they never gave her a compliment.

Or, if family members felt jealous of your beauty, they would gleefully point out any flaws in your appearance and mock you for them. Out of self-defense, a lovely little girl might grow up wearing shapeless clothes and cutting her own hair with nail scissors to avoid the spotlight of shame she feels sure awaits her whenever other people look at her.

Alternatively, you might come from a culture that avoids praising its children—a custom born of an ancient superstition that jealous gods will snatch away bright or beautiful youngsters.

In this case, if a stranger says, "What a fine-looking child!" a protective mother will protest, "No! You can't mean this ugly little monkey. She scares the birds out of the trees!"

The mother downplays her child's charms because, consciously or unconsciously, she wants to keep her youngster safe from any marauding gods roaming the neighborhood.

But what the daughter remembers all her life is that her mother called her an ugly little monkey. And that is how she will see herself, regardless of what others see when they look at her.

Reason #3 Why It's Hard to See Your Own Beauty

Your DNA shapes the way you see yourself

Your genes carry all the emotions, thoughts, beliefs, experiences, memories, and judgments of your forebears—including your mother and father. Your DNA can be considered a biological manifestation of eternal life. The beliefs, habits, hurts, and joys of ancestors who lived centuries ago still live within you.

So, it's not just you in there, inside your skin. Which is why it can be so hard to rid yourself of painful habits, thoughts, emotions, behavioral patterns, or beliefs. They've been tattooed on your genes since time out of mind and, in some cases, reinforced by the family you grew up with.

For this reason, addictions, negativity, hopelessness, or anxiety may feel like they are part of who you are—even though they are not and never can be. Who you truly are is so much more beautiful, strong, and wise than you may be able to perceive at the moment.

Some of the most common confidence-wrecking beliefs held in the DNA include:

"I am unwanted."

"I am an accident."

"I am a mistake."

"I am unlovable."

"It is wrong for me to be here."

These unconscious programs have been carried by billions of babies born to parents who did not want or love them. Children born to such parents often grow up thinking, "My folks don't love me. It must be because I'm unlovable."

It makes sense, as far as it goes. After all, your parents know you better than anyone. It seems reasonable that if they don't love you, it must be because there is something wrong with you. It's a natural outgrowth of the innocent egotism of childhood that believes "Everything happens because of me."

With an "I am the center of the universe" mentality, an unloved child finds it difficult to imagine that Mother or Father may not love or want her because they are incapable of love. Or because their child is too much, or too little, like them. Or because one or both parents grew up in a house where abandonment, rage, manipulation, shame, or neglect passed for love, and it's all they know.

When you feel unlovable, it's hard to love yourself. Your body. Or your life. It feels weird to picture good things coming into your life if you feel unworthy of having them. Your innate sense of fairness forbids you to receive more than you feel you deserve.

And yet, you are immensely lovable, in all your beauty and vulnerability and deep humanity. I love you right now, and I'm not the only one. To see you succeed in your creative business would fill me, and many others, with profound joy.

You are immensely lovable, in all your beauty and vulnerability and deep humanity.

The Good News

Your DNA is not your destiny. You have free will. You can choose to change the way you see yourself at any time by praying for the miracle of right perception. Ask to see yourself and your body in a new light.

On the scientific front, research by evolutionary biologist Dr. Bruce Lipton and neuroscientist Dr. Joe Dispenza shows that we can turn certain genes on and off with conscious intention and by changing our behavior, proving that it's possible to alter your genetic blueprint.

Just as you are more than your body, you are bigger than your DNA.

More Good News

Some of the most tormenting thoughts in your head may not even be yours.

They might come from a parent, sibling, childhood friend, bully, teacher, or other authority figure in your life.

They could be echoes from ancestors who lived generations ago.

They might have been spoken by a doctor or nurse attending your birth, and your brain recorded it.

These are all good reasons for making a practice of questioning painful thoughts instead of taking them as gospel truth.

Rather than allowing feelings of self-doubt or self-hatred to distress you, you can look upon them as old hurts coming up to be healed. Whether the issues are yours or an ancestor's, they can still be resolved and released with love, compassion and respect.

A Simple Way to Neutralize Upsetting Thoughts and Feelings

When you realize a hurtful thought or painful feeling is coming up, take a deep breath.

Notice the thought or feeling without getting caught up in its drama. Take another deep breath.

*Notice the thought or feeling without
getting caught up in its drama.*

Picture the thought or feeling as a dark cloud floating across the blue sky of your mind. Take a third deep breath.

Say to the cloud, "Hello" or "I see you." Then picture the cloud floating over the horizon, never to be seen again.

If you like, take another deep breath and blow the cloud on its way. Watch it fly away until it vanishes.

Notice how you feel. Keep on breathing.

Appreciate yourself for treating yourself with love and compassion.

Rinse and repeat as needed.

You can honor the ancestors living in your DNA without having to carry around their emotional or mental burdens. Instead, you can create the soul-satisfying life they hoped their descendants would enjoy. Your success will be the answer to their prayers.

My prayer: that you will find inspiration in these pages for making small, loving changes in the way you treat yourself and your body.

Let's begin by looking at how your feelings about your body affect your ability to succeed as a creative woman entrepreneur.

Why Respecting Your Body Matters in Your Business

Your body is your company's most important asset.

Without a body in good working order, it's hard for you and your dream business to thrive.

Your body is your company's most important asset.

It serves you as a person, as well as a business owner, to make physical well-being one of your top priorities.

If you create healthy habits now, they will be part of your routine when clients or customers start clamoring for your attention. This makes it easier to continue leading a balanced life as your business blossoms.

If you've already launched your business, you know how exhausting it can be. Honoring your physical self by cultivating healthy habits will help your body renew itself.

If your company exists mostly in your imagination right now, it's important to realize that starting a real-world business uses a tremendous amount of physical, mental, emotional, and spiritual energy.

That's because you're fighting the gravitational pull of ingrained habits and daily routines.

If you're like many creative women, you're also struggling with feelings of unworthiness or inadequacy. You may even unconsciously fear success, failure, acceptance, or rejection, among other things.

Internal conflicts like these create the "one foot on the brakes, one foot on the gas" condition that life coaches talk about. They keep you stuck.

They can even make you sick. High-intensity emotions, conflicting desires, and mental struggles can lead to physical debility because they weaken your immune system. They can also distract you when you're out walking, driving, or traveling—making you more prone to accidents and injuries.

Oddly enough, when you treat your body with respect and care, you tend to feel better emotionally. You think more clearly. It's easier to focus. Chalk it up to the mind/body connection. When you care for your body, that caring heals your heart and mind, too.

So, cultivating wholesome habits pays dividends:

Physically – When you feel good, it frees you to pay attention to what matters most to you: your creative muse, your clients, your latest project, leading your people, or _____ (you fill in the blank).

Financially – The healthier you are, the more likely you are to see a robust bottom line in your business. It's hard to be productive when you're sick or stressed.

Emotionally – It's easier to give your business, as well as your clients, the attention and care they deserve when you're not wrestling with out-of-control feelings.

Mentally – You get more done when your mind has the clarity and focus you need to take care of business—both professionally and personally.

Spiritually – Having faith in yourself, and in the value of what you offer, comes more naturally when you feel healthy and whole.

Honoring your body energizes you on all of these levels.

Why It's Hard to Take Care of Your Body

Having spent seven years in bed with a back injury, I know first-hand how hard it is to get around without a working spine. How challenging it can be to launch and run a business when you can only stay vertical for 15 minutes a day because of chronic pain and weakness. How discouraging it is when your biggest accomplishment of the last seven days was taking a shower.

In short, life and business without a functional body can be tough going.

And yet, many people seem to regard physical self-care as a chore they'll get around to someday when they're in the mood. Maybe.

Reasons for ignoring the body until something goes wrong include:

Being Too Busy

"I don't have time!" stands as one of the primary reasons women give for neglecting physical self-care.

It's a legitimate reason, as far as it goes. Time is your most limited resource. You live in a busy world that's just getting busier. Demands on your time, money, energy, and attention pile up until you're staggering under the weight of the obligations you've taken on.

When you start your own business, you will have even more activities on your plate. You will need to do sales and marketing; open a shop of the online or brick-and-mortar variety; create products, services, or offers of some kind; serve your clients; and, oh yes, have a life beyond your business.

All this hustle and bustle can drain a person dry, to the point where you decide to close up shop. You and your dreams deserve better than that.

Lack of Self-Esteem

It's easy to spot a woman who feels unloved or unlovable.

She walks around looking like an unmade bed.

None of her clothes quite fit. Her hair smells musty. If she's bothered to put on make-up, the lipstick or mascara looks smeared.

When you're going through a rough time, it's perfectly normal to let yourself go. All your attention goes to trying to survive. Even the most basic elements of self-care can fall by the wayside when you're caught up in a crisis.

But if you look like an unmade bed every day ... if surviving your life consumes every ounce of your energy ... I have been there. Done that. Bought the underwear.

And I am here to tell you that barely scraping by is no fun.

There is much more to life than simple survival. Survival is meant to be the starting point of your existence. Not the goal.

From a business standpoint, it's worth realizing that when potential clients see signs of self-neglect, many figure that you will neglect them, too. They will give their business to someone who looks and acts like she respects herself, knowing she will treat them with respect, too.

Equating Self-Care With Selfishness

If you're like most women, you have been trained to put the needs of others before your own.

I've worked with women who push themselves to the point of collapse rather than risk being labeled as selfish or uncaring by their loved ones.

The tendency toward self-sacrifice can reveal itself in subtler ways, too:

Let's say you're excited about seeing a new movie, but the friend coming with you wants to go to a different film. You give in without a murmur and go with your friend's choice, even though you're seething with resentment.

Maybe you're cross-eyed from lack of sleep, but Mom needs you to drive her somewhere. You suck it up and take her where she needs to go, grinding your teeth all the way.

Perhaps you've received upsetting news and you need a few minutes to pull yourself together before getting on with work. But your boss needs you in his office right now, so to his office you go. You feel too scattered to pay attention to what he's saying and so you miss something important.

If this sounds like you, you're probably running on empty right now.

Maybe you even feel angry sometimes, wondering when someone will consider your needs as thoughtfully as you consider the needs of others.

Putting others first is a great way to show your love for those you care about. But you deserve to show yourself love, too.

Consider this: those who end up collapsing from exhaustion will be unable to take care of anyone, including themselves.

Living in Your Head

Maybe you're one of those dynamic, creative women who can't be bothered to eat regular meals or go to sleep once inspiration strikes. You pull all-nighters. You eat a snack every few days if you think of it. You only stop when you can't do anything more because you love being in the creative flow.

It's like you're a brain walking on two legs.

If that sounds like you—well, it sounds like me, too, back in the day. There's nothing I love more than living in the flow. It's one of the reasons I continue to run my own business. It fills me with joy to commune with the inspired spirit driving my work.

As wonderful as the creative process is, it will take your body down if you overdo it. As you age (or at least, as *I* age), the body finds it harder to function on insufficient sleep and food. Exercise is essential, too, because the older you get, the more your body becomes a use-it-or-lose-it proposition.

It pays to take care of your one and only body—in business and in life.

It pays to take care of your one and only body
—in business and in life.

Living in Your Feelings

If you're like many creative women, you have moods. Sometimes you're up. Sometimes you're down. Sometimes you're brimming with energy. Sometimes you wake up feeling like your body has been glued to the mattress.

When your emotions get in a whirl, they pick you up and carry you along until they've exhausted themselves—and you.

All this turmoil can make physical self-care a hit-or-miss affair.

Whether upsetting emotions prompt you to cram cookies into your mouth by the handful, starve yourself until your hipbones stick out like a picket fence, or drink until you pass out—it takes a tremendous toll on your body.

Letting your feelings run the show takes a toll on your business, too. One of the crucial elements of success is consistency. It's vital to show up every day, not just when you're in the mood. Clients and customers want someone they can count on.

One of the crucial elements of success is consistency.

How to Build Honoring Your Body into Your Business

With all the stuff you have to do to get your creative business up and running, it can be tempting to put off physical self-care until things slow down.

Trouble is, if business slows down, you're likely to work twice as hard to get things moving again.

That's why it's important to build body care into your business sooner rather than later.

The self-care habits you form in the early days of your business tend to become part of your routine. Having healthy habits in place frees you to turn your attention to other matters, like how you can make more money doing something you love.

So, it can be beneficial to start practicing good self-care habits right now. They will stand you in good stead for the rest of your life.

Here are some suggestions.

Make Your Workplace Comfortable

If you spend a lot of time on the computer, consider getting an ergonomic chair and keyboard. It also helps to use eyeglasses—prescription or generic—that filter blue light, to avoid eyestrain from long hours of looking at a computer screen. Take time to get up and stretch every hour or so, just to get the blood flowing again.

If you're on your feet for most of your workday, invest in comfortable, well-fitting shoes and support hosiery. Remember to stretch your spine at the end of the day.

Drink as much water as you can while on the job. Hydration boosts your brain function. It also flushes out your organs, which keeps them in good working order.

Take frequent breaks to keep your mind sharp and your body functioning at an optimum level. If you can take a full lunch hour, with a walk and a nourishing meal, go for it.

Honor Your Body's Rhythms

Notice when you feel most energetic during the day. These will be your most productive hours. Knowing this helps you to choose your working hours. (This is one of my favorite things about having my own business.)

Honoring your body's rhythms also helps you make the best use of your time each day.

For instance, if you feel most inspired at night, set aside those hours for creative work. Be sure to give yourself time to sleep late the next day. Make your business appointments for the afternoon or evening, so you can show up as your best self.

If you're a morning person, do your most creative or demanding tasks as early in the day as possible. Save afternoons for tasks you find easy. Set aside your evenings for rest or play, depending on what works best for you.

Plan Meals and Snacks in Advance

When you're in the creative flow, it's a bummer to have to stop and figure out what to eat when you get hungry.

Sending out for pizza or take-out looks like an easy solution, but your body pays a high price for that convenient carton of fat, salt, sugar, and unhealthy carbohydrates.

One simple solution is to take an hour on your day off to put together healthy lunches and snacks for the next few days.

When hunger strikes, you have something ready to pull out of the refrigerator. You don't have to lose your creative buzz by thinking about food because it's already there waiting for you.

And, your body gets the nourishment it needs. You save money. Your brain gets the nutrients it needs. Your body feels like you care about it. Your hips might even slim down. What's not to love?

Create a Signature Look

As a creative businesswoman, you are your brand. The face and voice of your company.

One way to make you and your business more memorable is a distinctive personal style

You could make hats your trademark, or dramatic scarves, eye-catching glasses, one striking piece of jewelry, a favorite color you wear everywhere.

*As a creative businesswoman,
you are your brand.*

With all the allergy-prone folks out there, you would do well to avoid using a signature fragrance. Just smell clean.

Your professional image can be as one-of-a-kind as you are. In fact, uniqueness is a plus in most creative fields. You don't have to look like anyone else.

Taking the time to look your best helps you attract top-notch clients, customers, partners, investors, and mentors.

Looking good makes you feel good. It gives you confidence. And confidence is like catnip to prospective clients.

Pro tip: if you offer softer services, like life coaching or healing, consider dressing in a way that looks clean and professional. This will automatically make you stand out from flaky folks in your line of work.

The more professional you look—regardless of your field—the more people will trust you and want to do business with you.

How Physical Self-Care Transformed Me and My Business

Low energy, brain fog, and general listlessness made it hard to get my business going again after my big financial crash in 2010.

Adding to the difficulty in rebuilding my company: two surgeries to remove glands that govern the endocrine system and metabolism. The procedures left me too exhausted to leave my bed on most days.

My writing dried up because I had nothing to say.

My healing and coaching practice only consisted of a few regular clients because I had no energy to market my services to new prospects.

In short, things looked dire. My company's biggest asset—me—was down. And so was my revenue.

It became clear I had to focus first on health, so I would then have the energy to restart my business.

Hormone replacement therapy wasn't an option, for medical reasons. Neither was asking my doctor for pep pills, because I didn't want to risk becoming dependent on prescription drugs.

I tried energy drinks, smart water, Vitamin B12, Chinese herbs, and supplements to support the adrenaline and immune systems. None of them worked for very long, if at all.

I lacked the energy to do exercises that would build up my stamina

I was stymied. What else could I do?

Hmm. Maybe my diet needed overhauling. I ate healthy-ish, but still allowed myself a fancy coffee drink with whipped cream once a week.

A friend suggested trying "The Fast Metabolism Diet" by Haylie Pomroy. It required a major lifestyle change, but I was willing to give it a month's trial.

Within 30 days, I lost seven pounds. My waist and hips looked slimmer. My cravings stopped. Best of all, my energy started coming back.

After reaching my goal weight, I decided to stay with the program simply because it makes me feel strong and healthy.

The increased energy made it possible to resume exercising, enhancing my sense of well-being. And my productivity at work has never been higher.

While this diet program works for me, it's not for everyone. We're all different.

The point is, I didn't quit until I found something that works for me. And you can do the same.

It pays to discover what will give you the strength, stamina, and energy to build your dream business, and live your dream life.

You've Got This

It's never too late to start honoring your body by practicing physical self-care.

Whatever condition your body is in, it has the power to heal itself in ways that science is only beginning to understand.

Whatever condition your body is in, here you are, reading this book about finding the confidence to start or expand your own creative business.

The very act of reading these words proves that you have strength and courage.

Proves that you're not done yet.

Proves that you have depths within you still untapped.

Building your dream business is a great way to discover how smart, how special, and how mighty you truly are.

And whether your business ends up going north, south, or sideways—the woman you become as you build it is a person you can take pride in.

You become a woman who walks tall. Stands strong. Loves fiercely. And creates joyfully.

Let's keep going, shall we?

You become a woman who walks tall.
Stands strong. Loves fiercely.
And creates joyfully.

Cherish Your Spirit

"You are the light of the world."

—A Course in Miracles

Why Cherishing Your Spirit Matters in Your Business

It's a blessing that you've chosen to share your gifts in a way that allows you to prosper, as well as those you serve.

This is why your talents were given to you. You're meant to share them. Otherwise, your gifts would have been given to someone else.

Nothing says you have to give away your offerings for free. You can if you want to, of course. But it's not a requirement. You can express your creative vision and make money from it, too.

Nothing says you have to give away your gifts for free.

There is a reason why you picked up this book. You and I have had this appointment for a long time. Thank you for showing up.

Why You Want To Start a Business

Let's take a moment to consider why you want to channel your creativity into a business where you're paid to share the fruits of your imagination.

Maybe you're sick of working for other people who don't appreciate you or value what you have to offer. That is totally legitimate. Good for you.

Perhaps you feel under-employed—that your job or career uses only a tenth of all that you have to offer—and you want to give more. How fortunate for all of us if you feel that way. We've been waiting a long time for you to share your gifts, my friend.

Possibly you're frustrated because you're filled with creative ideas, but you don't have the time or energy to develop them. They remain orphaned children begging for your love and attention. You want to give them full rein to run and play and shout or sing. So, if you could do creative work full-time, how fulfilling would that be?

Whatever has been encouraging you to step up and share your gifts as a creative professional, your spirit is the force behind it.

Where Your Spirit Fits Into Your Work

Your spirit comprises your dreams and desires, your imagination, your intuition, and your free will. It is your essential you-ness as a human being who is also one with Infinite Love.

Your spirit serves your soul. Think of it this way: your soul (the eternal part of you) has checked into a hotel (your body) for a time. Your spirit acts as your soul's personal concierge of this hotel, devoted to making sure the soul has everything it needs to carry out the purpose of its visit, before your soul goes on to the next adventure.

So, if your spirit has been urging you to devote more time and energy to nurturing and expressing your creativity, it's because your soul has plans. Big plans. And they involve you getting out there as a creative professional.

Here's the thing: if this desire has been planted in you, you have also been given the means to make it happen.

Your soul would never torture you by making you want something with all your heart and then tell you, "You can't have it." It knows your Higher

Your soul has plans. Big plans.

Power wants for you what you want for yourself. How great is it to know that the Divine is on your side? That Life Itself encourages your success?

By contrast, your ego-mind can withhold approval, love, and support from you all day long.

Where the Ego-Mind Takes You Down

The ego-mind is the part of you that believes you are separate from all that is. It's a necessary part of your make-up, since it helps you perceive the difference between "me" and "not-me." This keeps your sense of self intact.

If something or someone has crushed your spirit, your ego-mind may have plopped itself into the captain's chair because, hey, someone's got to steer your ship if your life force has gone AWOL.

When your ego-mind does the navigating, it plays tricks on you, such as:

Tormenting you with deep longings for someone or something unattainable.

Dangling an exciting prospect in front of you and then snatching it away.

Delivering exactly what you want and then sabotaging it.

Getting you hooked on hopelessness or helplessness or "The Jerry Springer Show."

Why does it do this? Because it can.

The job of the unchecked ego-mind is not to make you happy. Its job is to keep you off-balance, so it can dominate you.

Which is why your creative business needs to be rooted in your spirit's quest to help your soul fulfill its purpose.

No need to throw your ego overboard. Put it in the crow's nest, where it can keep an eye out for stormy weather.

When you honor your spirit by putting it in the captain's chair, it becomes easier to trust yourself. To move forward in faith and stay the course. To commit to something that brings you joy, meaning, success and satisfaction—like your creative business.

Four Reasons Why It's Hard to Cherish Your Spirit

Feelings of Unworthiness

Of all the sneaky ploys of the ego-mind, one of its most devastating is the faux spirituality that says, "Believing that I'm unworthy or undeserving proves that I'm a good person."

This mentality can be fatal to your business's bottom line. Feelings of unworthiness chase away potential clients faster than a hungry bear on the rampage.

Low self-worth makes you feel guilty about saying "No" to things you don't want to do, because you believe that other people's wants and needs matter more than yours.

A sense of "I am not enough" pressures you to give clients, colleagues and loved ones all your time, money, energy and caring—until you're broke, burned out, or both.

When a prospective customer gets a whiff of your unworthiness energy, chances are she will:

- Demand a discount on your work
- Push for a jumbo-size free sample of what you offer
- Claim that she can't afford you, so you should lower your rates—and you cave in because you're sorry for her or desperate for business

And if you agree to work together, chances are she'll be an aggravating, time-sucking, energy-draining nightmare of a client.

Feelings of being undeserving are contagious. If you feel like you are not good enough, most potential customers will agree that you're not up to the job, which prompts them to hire someone who is possibly less talented but definitely more confident than you.

Here's the thing:

It's impossible for you to be unworthy. You are valuable beyond imagining and loved beyond measure. There is nothing you need to prove. Worthiness is not earned. It is revealed.

Worthiness is not earned. It is revealed.

A person can waste her life trying to validate her value to herself, to her loved ones, or to her clients and colleagues.

It never works.

That's because the ego-mind that tells you you're not good enough is the *same* ego-mind that will never accept anything you do as good enough. Finding fault is its job. It does this to keep you from feeling too good about yourself, because it believes it will die if you start trusting yourself more than you trust your critical inner voice.

The truth is, the ego-mind will survive if you gain confidence in yourself. It will simply change position in your consciousness, from the driver's seat to the back seat. From there, your ego-mind can watch your back, which is its job.

To start, ask your Higher Power for right perception of who you really are. Of why it is safe for you to recognize your true worth now. Of why you deserve love, riches, recognition, respect, and all else that you desire.

Once you get out from under the tyranny of "not good enough," it's easier to feel free to build a business you love.

To work with people you love, who adore working with you.

To charge a generous fee for your amazing work.

To respectfully set strong boundaries so you can protect your valuable time, energy, and financial security.

To form alliances and partnerships with gifted people of integrity, so you can expand your empires together.

With a healthy sense of self-worth, you can build success and satisfaction into your creative business right from the start.

To paraphrase Jacob Glass, you don't get the business you deserve; you get the business you think you deserve.

Look, you deserve the best, most successful, and fulfilling business possible. Not because you're talented, beautiful, and creative—even though you are—but simply because you exist. You are the one and only *you*, a precious gem beyond compare.

Inability to Imagine Anything Better for Yourself

As a creative woman, you have plenty of imagination. This is one of your greatest assets in creating a successful and satisfying business. It helps you in doing your work, in promoting your offerings in ingenious ways, and in setting the foundation of the business itself.

Everything ever made by humans begins with imagination. A woman has an idea for a video, and then she makes the video. A man gets an idea for a story, and then he writes the story. You get the idea.

But if all that you can imagine for yourself is failure, frustration, or struggle in your business—that is what you will experience. Welcome to the dark side of the law of attraction.

Sometimes we get what we want, but more often we get what we expect.

So, it's essential to adjust your expectations accordingly. Aim for the stars, rather than what you think is possible or do-able or sensible.

Choose to expect success and prosperity.

Choose to expect that you and your work will be in demand.

Choose to expect high-quality clients who can't stop raving about you.

Instead of using your imagination to envision all the things that could go wrong, picture yourself enjoying success and soul-satisfaction—whatever that means to you.

Let's say you'd like your business to take you all over the world, where you can meet new people, enjoy new adventures, and see amazing sights.

Or perhaps you have a dream home you'd love to live in: a cozy nest, a soothing sanctuary, a marble mansion graced with fine art, an aerie on a mountaintop, or a cottage by the sea.

You might joyfully anticipate sharing your wealth with your loved ones, or the less fortunate, or causes you care about, like saving animals in shelters, or supporting women running for office.

Or possibly you would love it if your work attracted a partner who is perfect for you, and you build a loving life together as well as a thriving business.

Hold your dreams in your imagination. Then get to work.

Hold your dreams in your imagination.
Then get to work.

Lack of Faith in Yourself

If you're like many creative women, you grew up in a family that thought creativity was for men … or for idiots … or okay for a hobby, but certainly nothing you could turn into a profitable business.

You might even have had a loved one tell you, "You've got to forget these crazy dreams. Get practical. Train as a teacher, or something else you can fall back on."

Loved ones usually believe they do this because they love you, and that may be true, as far as it goes.

But the fact is, they're crushing your spirit to spare you from getting crushed later. Better, they reason, to kill your dreams before you invest time and energy and money into a venture they believe will fail.

This is pure insanity. Whether your spirit gets crushed now or later— what's the difference?

All they're doing is projecting their disappointments onto you. In fact, their tribulations have nothing to do with you or what is possible for you.

They'll tell you that no one makes money writing—discounting successful authors from Charlotte Brontë and Virginia Woolf to J.K. Rowling, Amy Tan, and Maya Angelou.

They'll tell you artists are always broke, as if Mary Cassatt, Georgia O'Keefe, Frida Kahlo, and Judy Chicago were chopped liver.

They'll tell you no one makes money from music—forgetting about Ethel Waters, Doris Day, Dolly Parton, Madonna, Gloria Estefan, Beyoncé and Ariana Grande.

They'll tell you no one makes it in movies, theater, or television—as if Shonda Rhimes, Salma Hayek, Julie Taymor, Patty Jenkins, Lucy Liu, and Oprah Winfrey never existed.

They'll tell you there's no money in life or business coaching—ignoring Martha Beck, Suze Orman, Marie Kondo, Lisa Nichols, Jen Sincero, and Marisa Murgatroyd.

They'll tell you intuitive healers never make a dime—overlooking Louise Hay, Doreen Virtue, Colette Baron-Reid, Caroline Myss, Judith Orloff, and Mona Lisa Schulz.

Part of the problem: Your loved one may view celebrities as beings apart from mere mortals. And if family members have known you since you were in diapers, they can have a hard time picturing you as someone who belongs in the firmament of the famous.

So, instead of waiting until others believe in you, you need to be the first to have faith in yourself and your work.

When you believe in yourself, other people start to do the same. And that is how you build your successful and satisfying business, one delighted client at a time.

*When you believe in yourself, other people
start to do the same.*

Reluctance to Receive

Almost all of the women I've worked with who struggle to start or sustain a business have one thing in common:

They have a hard time with receiving.

These generous souls will give until they bleed. But taking is another story.

Trouble with receiving can reveal itself in subtle ways, such as:

Turning away compliments: "What, this old thing?" or "I was just in the right place at the right time."

Refusing assistance: "Thanks, but I can get the door myself" or "No, I'll figure it out on my own."

Under-charging for your services: "I'm not good enough yet to charge as much as other people do" or "My clients can only afford so much. If I raise my rates, I'll lose them!"

Giving away too much: "I'm offering prospective clients a free one-hour sample session" or "I've put together a series of free training videos and I'm following that up with a free webinar"

Declining payment or reimbursement: "Oh, no, I couldn't charge you for that" or "You don't have to repay me. You need the money more than I do."

Easy come, easy go: Every time you get a financial windfall, the money quickly evaporates, thanks to an emergency or an impulsive spending spree. Why is that? The extra money pushed you out of your financial comfort zone, so the universe lovingly helped you get rid of the excess cash as quickly as possible.

On the spiritual level, a reluctance to receive reflects a belief in scarcity. There is not enough love. Not enough money. Not enough time. Not enough energy.

Basically, there is not enough *good* to go around, so someone has to go begging. That would be you.

And that belief will keep you struggling until you and your business go under financially.

Scarcity thinking can also keep you stuck in an unsatisfying romantic relationship (if you have one).

Shut down your creativity.

Disconnect you from your intuition.

Even compromise your health.

Because what you focus on expands. In this instance, you're focusing on not-enoughness—so you get more not-enoughness. Some fun.

Furthermore, many belief systems, cultures, and religions declare that if you're poor, it must be the will of God. Or that you have to be poor to be close to God.

If you commit the sin of getting rich, God will strike you down or send you to perdition.

In cases like these, staying poor understandably looks safer than the perils prosperity can bring.

If you happened to be born into a wealthy family, maybe you grew up feeling guilty about being rich. You can't give away your money fast enough because you want to gain favor in God's eyes and ease your conscience.

Taking less so others can have more may seem like a good way to live. It is, unless you take it to extremes of self-deprivation.

You cannot be so poor it will make someone else rich. You cannot be so successful it will cause others to fail. You cannot be so loved that others must live without affection. You cannot be so fulfilled that it will use up all the satisfaction available to others.

In short, it's impossible to be "too rich," "too successful," or "too happy" unless you decide it is.

We live in a universe overflowing with abundance. Anyone looking for it can find it. And it is available to anyone who is willing to receive it.

That's the trick. You have to be open to recognizing, accepting, and receiving the good that is all around you.

It's impossible to do this for anyone else. Opening to receive is an inside job.

You can set an example by saying, as true spiritual leaders do: "I'll go first."

By claiming the good that is your birthright, you empower others to do the same. That way, everyone prospers—including you.

By claiming the good that is your birthright, you empower others to do the same.

You can start by:

Accepting compliments: "Thank you, I love this outfit" or "Thanks, I worked hard for that promotion."

Allowing assistance: "Thanks, please hold the door for me" or "Yes, I'd love it if you'd help me figure this out."

Charging appropriately for your services: "I'd love to work with you. The hourly rate is $___. How would you like to pay?" or "So glad you like it! It's only $___. Do you want to pay by credit card or cash?" Fill in the $___ with rates that cover your time and costs, with enough extra for you to make a profit.

Giving away just enough: "I'm offering prospective clients a free 15-minute consultation" or "I've put together a free training video and I'm following that up with a paid webinar series."

Accepting payment or reimbursement: "Thank you. I appreciate it."

Using windfalls wisely: "I'm going to save a third of this extra money, spend a third of it, and invest a third of it in myself, my business, or my portfolio."

Five Ways to Honor Your Spirit by Allowing Success

Make Peace With the Past

If you're like most creative women, you spend a lot of time living in your imagination.

You think about creative projects you did in the past, the work you're doing now, and the projects you plan to undertake in the future—which is awesome.

What's not so awesome: dwelling on upsetting experiences in the past.

Look, it's normal to think about the things that went wrong for you. And you naturally want to avoid repeating the hurts and mistakes of the past.

But looking to the past to help you avoid future pain never works. All it does is project the past into the future. Your future then takes shape accordingly.

You have the power to influence the way your future unfolds, through your free will. Through your intentions. Through your choices. Most of all, through your actions.

No one can foretell the way the future will unfold, because it hinges on multiple factors beyond your awareness. It's impossible to take into account possibilities that you cannot see or foresee. But you can do your best, and that in itself brings rewards beyond imagining.

If or when you're ready to make peace with the past, you can lay the groundwork for a richly fulfilling future by making choices like these:

Accept that an upsetting event happened. Acceptance doesn't mean it's okay with you. It just means you're acknowledging "It happened" instead of insisting "It shouldn't have happened" or "It wasn't supposed to work out that way."

Bless all concerned. Forget about forgiving others, for now. Just wish them well. Bless yourself, too.

Stop ill-wishing others. Mentally cursing people keeps your wounds fresh while draining your energy, focus, and will.

Let go of your urge for revenge. Physical, emotional, financial, or verbal violence only begets more violence.

Build a life and business you love, one inspired action at a time. Living well is truly the best revenge.

When you close your heart against anyone or anything, you close it against everyone and everything, because we are all one. You can't pick and choose, "I'll open to this but not that." Oneness doesn't work that way. It's all about inclusion.

When you choose to forgive, you open up your life to new possibilities, new opportunities, and new love.

When you choose to forgive, you open up your life to new possibilities, new opportunities, and new love.

Live in Your Body

I see many creative women who imagine a world filled with love, beauty, truth, wisdom, generosity, peace, harmony, and joy.

If imagination were all it took to be effective in daily life, these women would be ruling the planet by now—and doing a great job of it.

Instead, they're struggling.

Their difficulty—and perhaps yours—lies in living more in the imagination than in the present moment. Thoughts about the past or the future occupy most of your waking moments, while what's happening now barely registers on your radar.

I get it. If you grew up in a dysfunctional family, your imagination likely provided refuge from intolerable circumstances you were too young to escape. Psychologists call it dissociation—the separation of portions of your consciousness or personality from your main sense of identity. It's hard to feel whole or confident when part of you is here and other parts of you are somewhere else.

If you live more in your imagination than what passes for the real world, please know that doing so helped you develop your creative gifts. Your intuition. Your insight. Your intelligence. Your compassion for the suffering of others. Your desire for a world rich in love and understanding.

In short, you have done nothing wrong by dwelling so much in your thoughts and feelings.

I'm just saying the rest of you needs love and attention, too.

Your body needs nourishment, sleep, water, movement, and affection.

Your bank account needs money consistently coming in.

And your business, if you want it to be satisfying and successful, needs to attract and keep first-class clients and customers.

The key to being more effective in the day-to-day world is mindfulness. Be here now.

The key to being more effective in the
day-to-day world is mindfulness.

Let your awareness or spirit fully occupy your body, from the top of your head to the tips of your toes and fingers.

Pay attention to what happens in your body and attend to it.

Be aware of the people and the environment around you.

Focus on giving your best to what is in front of you right now. Let the past recede into the past where it belongs. Choose to trust the future will take care of itself while you focus on this moment.

Your efforts may or may not bring the results you intended, but you will love the person you become as you take one inspired action after another.

Be True to Yourself

The greatest regret of the dying, according to hospice studies, involves having lived the life that someone else wanted for them, rather than the life they themselves wanted.

In other words, they valued the dreams and needs of others more than they valued their own. And as their last days played out, they wished they had been true to themselves.

It's not too late for you. You still have time to start noticing whose dreams you are working to turn into a reality.

If you realize you have been trying to please someone else, it's okay. It happens.

Women throughout history have been trained to please others rather than please themselves. Otherwise, they risked being labeled selfish or uncaring. They risked losing love, or even their lives.

Out of misguided loyalty to your loved ones, you may have taken on the task of living out their frustrated dreams by starting a job, career, or business that makes *them* happy—but not you.

It probably seemed like a good idea at the time.

Maybe you did it because you wanted to heal them or please them or make them love you—all natural and legitimate concerns.

Perhaps you did it because your family pestered you to do what they wanted. You caved in out of a desire for peace at any price. You've forfeited the fulfillment of your dreams so others can feel better. Such sacrifice breeds resentment and turmoil, not peace.

Look, even if someone you love holds you responsible for their happiness, that can never *make* you responsible for their happiness, because joy is an inside job.

It's important to realize your spirit will keep after you until you do what you came here to do.

You are always free to make new choices and reap the rewards.

Choose to create a successful and soul-satisfying business. Buy your dream home. Treat yourself to a long-desired trip. Give your body, mind, heart, and soul the time and attention they need.

When you give yourself permission to do what you came here to do, the Universe starts lining up the resources you need to succeed. Support comes to you from unexpected sources. Investors pop up out of nowhere. Customers line up before you've even opened your doors.

You and your creative gifts are wanted. Needed. Gleefully anticipated.

From the standpoint of your spirit, sharing your talents is even more necessary for you than it is for those you serve. By sharing your authentic self, you honor the Divine.

Be bold. Dare to be true to yourself. It pays dividends beyond imagining.

Decide to Be Successful

Success is more than an experience. It is a decision.

You can make this choice at any time. How about now?

The sooner you decide that your creative business will be satisfying and successful, the sooner you will find yourself feeling more confident than ever before.

If that sounds crazy to you, consider this:

The physicist John Wheeler discovered that atoms are not so much teeny-tiny things as teeny-tiny tendencies. They're inchoate possibilities with the potential to turn into form and mass. In the meantime, atoms just hang out, winking in and out of existence faster than the speed of thought.

What makes atoms resolve into something solid and real, like the chair you're sitting on?

The power of decision.

The person who designed your chair felt inspired to create something people could sit on. She formulated ideas about the shape, size, colors, materials, and structure of this object. She designed it with conscious purpose. The folks who manufactured it set out to build this particular chair, rather than an evening gown or a space station. The chair found its way to you, and now you're sitting in it.

None of this happened by chance. One decision after another carried your chair from the imagination of the designer to you.

Likewise, you can choose to be successful rather than leaving it to chance or your horoscope or your score on a personality test.

Deciding to be successful harnesses the power of your will—a formidable force rooted in your spirit. It lassoes the atoms twinkling around you and starts forming them into the shape of your dreams and desires.

Pro tip: Be sure to envision your satisfying and successful business the way you want it, rather than the way you fear it will play out.

Every atom in the universe loves you to pieces. They will follow your lead wherever it takes them. If you direct the atoms toward struggling to build your business, you shall struggle.

If you direct your atoms toward success, get ready for the ride of a lifetime.

I've worked with many women who sabotaged their success because, consciously or unconsciously, they feared it would cost them something they value.

Some women worried about making more money than their father, which they believed would hurt or shame him.

Other women fretted about outshining their mother or daughter, especially if she works in the same field. They felt it would be wrong or bad or disloyal to be more successful, have more money, or be happier than their mother or their child.

Still others felt convinced that loved ones would resent their success and punish them for it with malicious gossip, by making outrageous emotional or financial demands, or by cutting off contact altogether.

In many cases, these are legitimate concerns.

Two things to consider:

Ask yourself why you give power over your life to folks who do not wish you well. If they are family members, think about spending less time with them and more time with those who support your dreams of a successful business.

If the ill-wishers are friends, you can widen your social circle to include people who want the best for you. Your dreams deserve support. It's up to you to make sure they get it.

While loved ones may feel threatened or aggrieved by your success, their upset happens on the personality level.

On the soul level, they say this prayer every day of their lives: "Dear Higher Power, please let my loved one (*that's you*) have a better life than I do."

Your triumph will be the answer to the prayer of their soul. And the fulfillment of your soul's purpose here on Earth.

So, I encourage you to align your atoms by deciding to have a successful and satisfying business—however that looks to you.

Abide by that decision every day, and you will be amazed by what shows up.

Here's the cool part: once you begin making decisions that support your good, you start seeing more success in your life and in your business right away. It doesn't take years to turn your ship around. When you start going in the right direction—shazam—you are going in the right direction.

Allow Yourself to Get Paid Well for Creative Work

I've worked with many women who deliberately or unconsciously under-charge for their work. The reasons they give include:

"I'm not good enough at what I do to charge more than I'm charging now."

"It's wrong to charge money for doing spiritual work. I shouldn't make people pay anything."

"What I do is creative. It's not real work, so how can I charge real money?"

"I'm not curing cancer here. No one's life is going to change because of something I do."

"Anyone can do what I do. I'm nothing special."

"It feels weird to make people pay for doing something that I would do for free."

"People who are much better at this work only charge $___."

"I know my work can make people's lives better, but I don't want to charge a fortune for it. I don't need to be rich. I just love doing the work."

"My sessions only run an hour. How can I justify charging $___ for sixty minutes of my time?"

The issues underlying these rationalizations for charging low or no fees for creative work include:

- Feeling unworthy or undeserving of one's good
- Confusing personal worth with the value of your work
- Fear or loathing of money

Let's explore these issues one at a time.

Feeling unworthy or undeserving of good reflects a deep-seated belief that there is not enough love, money, or good in general to go around. Someone has to do without so others can have more. In this case, that someone is you.

If you have this issue, it's not your fault. Your experiences in this life, as well as the society you grew up in and the history of humanity, have drummed a sense of scarcity into your bones.

Beliefs in lack and limitation hark from an ancient era. We're still pretty primitive, but more of us now understand that there is plenty of love, money, and good to go around. Unequal shares of good stem from lack of distribution, rather than lack of supply.

You have no reason to deny yourself proper payment for your wonderful work.

Anyone who excels at what they do—whether it's fixing plumbing, speaking wisdom, figuring taxes, or designing a website—deserves excellent pay. That includes you.

Confusing personal worth with the value of your work – Equating low income with low personal value and high income with high personal value has widespread currency. Maybe it's in the water. Perhaps it's in our DNA. Wherever it comes from, it permeates our society from top to bottom.

Look, on a personal level, your body is worth about $1.97 in chemicals. Your organs on the black market might fetch as much as $100,000, but you wouldn't be around to enjoy the money.

Your worth as a spiritual being in a human body is incalculable. You are rarer than the rarest diamond. Just by showing up, you make the world a better place.

Just by showing up,
you make the world a better place.

Your heart, mind, imagination, experience, education, intelligence, insight, and spirit are priceless. No one else can bring to the table what you can. It's only fair that people should pay top dollar for the fruits of your creative work. You are the only one who can provide the unique gifts you have to offer.

Fear or loathing of money – If you're one of the creative women who shrinks from money, who hates thinking about it, or who wishes she never had to deal with it—you have a lot of company. (You're probably broke, too. Money rarely goes where it's not wanted.)

For centuries, the poor have regarded the rich with mingled contempt and envy for their privileged lifestyle.

Religious leaders have taught that money, or love of money, is the root of all evil.

Rich people have tried to buy salvation by giving away their money.

Spiritual folks have virtuously avoided the corrupting influence of money, believing they must be poor to be close to God.

Thankfully, more of us are realizing that money is neither good nor bad, but neutral.

Money makes you more of who you are. It gives you more options and opportunities. It magnifies your you-ness.

If you are hard-wired for kindness—and you are, or you wouldn't be reading this book—wealth will never corrupt you. It will give you more ways to express your goodness. To lift up others. To give back. While being good to yourself, too.

Therefore, it is safe for you, safe for others, and safe for your immortal soul, for you to gain wealth through your creative genius.

You were not made to go begging through the world, being a burden to yourself, your family, or the state.

You were made to prosper.

One of the reasons you were given your creative talents is to support yourself financially.

You are free to decide how lavishly or modestly you live.

Just keep in mind, as the old gal said, "Whether you're rich or poor, it's nice to have money."

How Tina Found an Agent and Publisher

Tina came to me because she wanted to pave the way for success at the book expo in New York that she planned to attend the following day.

"I'm hoping to find an agent there," she said. "And I'd love it if I found a publisher, too."

Tina had her book proposal all set to go—an informative and entertaining sharing of her deep knowledge of her subject. It takes a lot of devotion to write a detailed book proposal. Tina had it in abundance. She knew her insights would help people. She wanted to get that book out there.

Despite her commitment and groundwork, Tina felt shaky about her prospects of finding a literary agent and publisher.

She knew she would attract higher quality people if she had more confidence in herself. But she couldn't get there on her own, which brought her to my office.

"The book expo is huge," Tina moaned. "And thousands of writers there want the same thing I want—an agent and a publisher. How do I compete? How can I boost my chances of finding what I'm looking for?"

"Try this out," I said. "How about deciding to find the ideal literary agent for you? How about choosing to find the perfect publisher for your book?"

Tina's blue eyes widened. "Can I *do* that?"

"Of course, you can," I said with a smile. "Your Higher Power wants for you what you want for yourself. Your will is God's will, and vice versa."

Tears began to stream down Tina's face.

"Okay," she whispered. "I am deciding right now to find the perfect agent and publisher for me."

We worked on the fears that came up once she voiced her choice. We wanted to ensure she could whole-heartedly stand by her decision.

By the end of the session, Tina confidently declared, "I am going to that expo and finding the best people to get my book out there!"

"Yes, you are," I affirmed.

She called two days later. "Oh my God, you're not going to believe this," Tina squealed.

"I met this fantastic agent as soon as I got off the plane in New York. He's huge in the industry! And he loved my book's concept. He couldn't wait to sign me!"

"That's wonderful!" I said. "Congratulations! You deserve it!"

"But there's more," Tina exulted. "We went to the expo together. He got **five publishers** interested in my book—*and* in my next projects!

"I know it's because of the work we did together," she added. "I cannot begin to thank you. You're amazing!"

I grinned through my tears of gratitude. "Right back at you, darling. We're both amazing."

Tina's new agent got her book published the next year. It received glowing reviews.

You Can Do It, Too

To find her perfect agent and publisher, Tina did everything that was hers to do.

She invested in her creative gifts by writing a smart, fun, and insightful book proposal about a popular topic.

She invested in her dream by buying a plane ticket and booking a hotel room so she could attend a major event to get her book out there, even though she felt intimidated by the prospect.

Instead of succumbing to doubt and fear, Tina invested in herself by hiring me to help her bring her "A" game to the Book Expo of America.

She went to New York to seize the opportunity she created for herself. And got a result even better than she imagined.

You can do the same, my friend.

As you build your satisfying and successful business, focus on doing what is yours to do.

Invest in developing and expressing your creative gifts.

Do your work with love, so the energy of your devotion permeates all that you create. Your clients, prospects, and colleagues will feel it and want more of what you have to offer.

Let go of merely hoping for the best. Step into your power by deciding to be successful.

Let go of merely hoping for the best.
Step into your power by deciding to be
successful.

Open to receive rightful compensation for the value you provide by sharing your unique creative vision.

Allow grateful clients and customers to shower you with money and appreciation.

You have it in you to do all this and more. I believe in you.

When you believe in yourself and in something greater than yourself, it lifts you to new heights of excellence and effectiveness in the world.

Find out more about that in the next chapter. Take my hand. We'll go there together.

Serve the Greater Good

"When I dare to be powerful—to use my strength in the service of my vision—then it becomes less and less important whether I am afraid."
—Audre Lord

Why Serving Something Greater Than Yourself Matters in Your Business

Starting and sustaining a business calls for vast quantities of time, energy, focus, commitment, persistence, and courage to keep it going.

If you're like most women, you can summon all these resources, and more, to help others. To help yourself or your business—not so much.

It feels right and natural to give your all for those you love.

It may feel wrong and unnatural to put great effort into something that benefits you alone.

Your brain has been hard-wired over millions of years to collaborate, cooperate, and sacrifice for the good of your tribe. To put the needs of others before your own, so the human race could survive and thrive.

It's hard to unhook yourself from behavioral patterns engraved in your DNA.

Fortunately, in this case, it's unnecessary.

Instead of forcing yourself into a "me first" attitude to do what needs to be done to create a satisfying and successful business, you have an alternative.

Explore the ways your work helps others.

Seeing how your creativity serves a greater good will elevate and enrich all that you do.

It makes you think better, because your brain functions best when performing actions that benefit society at large.

It satisfies your heart and soul, because understanding that your work has real value invests all your activities with meaning.

When you identify who you serve and how you serve them, it gets easier to summon the internal resources necessary to build a creative business that prospers everyone it touches—including you.

The way it works:

You've heard stories about mothers who lift five-ton trucks to rescue their child pinned beneath the vehicle. Even if the mother looks as fragile as a butterfly, she finds the strength to save her little one.

When you want to do something that deeply matters to you, you find a way to do it.

As you understand more clearly how valuable your creative work is for others, as well as for yourself, it gets easier to do what needs to be done to create your satisfying and successful business, like:

Allowing yourself to be visible. People like to see the face of the folks they are thinking of hiring. You need to make peace with being seen, heard, and listened to as you put yourself out there to inform, entertain, inspire, and/or educate your audience.

Setting prices that reflect the value of what you do and create financial security for you

Finding fun and easy ways to promote your business so more people know about you and your wonderful work

Creating a schedule that fits your body clock so you can do your work when you feel most creative or energized

Asking people for their business and being okay with the outcome either way

Creating products and/or services to offer to your people

Asking for payment and having the means to accept and process it (hello, PayPal!)

Tracking your income and expenses with a spreadsheet or bookkeeper

Hiring or partnering with people whose strong points balance your weak points and vice versa

Showing up when you say you will or rescheduling the appointment in a timely way

Devoting significant and satisfying time to doing the creative work you love to do

Enjoying a life beyond your business

Some of these activities will be easy for you, while others may challenge you.

Having one or two big, juicy, heartfelt reasons for turning your creative work into a business will help you stay the course.

The more deeply you connect your work with something greater than yourself, the more the universe will support you every step of the way.

While we're here, how about exploring your most compelling "Why" right now?

You can start by considering why you want to make a living doing creative work you love.

Write or draw any thoughts and feelings that come up as you ask yourself, "Why do I want to do my creative work for a living?"

Be honest with yourself. There are no wrong reasons for wanting to do what you love and get paid for it. And you are allowed to succeed, whatever that looks like to you.

Now, picture thousands of people clamoring for your creative offerings. See them happily paying top dollar for your work and bragging about you to their friends. Notice how imagining fame, fortune, and praise makes you feel. Observe your feelings without judging your emotions or yourself.

Take a moment now to reflect on what service means to you. Does the idea of service make you feel happy, or trapped, or something else? Again, be honest with yourself. There are no wrong answers here. Notice your emotions and thoughts without making them wrong, and without making yourself wrong for having them.

If service sounds like drudgery, slavery, or sacrifice to you, this would be a good moment to ask your Higher Power for right perception of service. You can also ask for right perception of yourself as one who serves. Notice what comes to mind. Sit in this awareness for as long as you like.

Next, you can consider ways that you would love to use your creative gifts to serve something greater than yourself in a way that also benefits you. Make a list, if you wish. For example, maybe you would love to lead workshops, do public speaking, travel for both business and pleasure, and mentor young people. Let your imagination play with the idea that it's possible to do things that are fun for you while spreading joy and making money. Remember: true service blesses both the server and the served.

*Remember: true service blesses both the
server and the served.*

In the light of your new awareness, you can ask yourself again, "Why do I want to build a business around my creativity?" See what comes up.

Then ask, "How grateful will I feel when I make a wonderful living doing what I love?" Notice the thoughts and feelings that come up. Marinate in any sense of joy, peace, or gratitude that arises. Draw or note down insights as they come to you if you want to remember them or use them in your daily life.

Good job!

When you're ready to move on, let's look at …

Five Reasons Why It's Hard to Connect With Something Greater Than Yourself

Distrust in Life

If you're like most people, you have experienced disappointment, hardship, betrayal, abandonment, rejection, regret, or defeat.

In short, sometimes life hasn't gone your way.

When bad things happen, it's normal to look upon life as something to be survived, rather than enjoyed. Or as something to hide from before it whacks you upside the head. Again.

Living a hard-knock life can make the idea of starting or expanding your own creative business seem like nothing short of insanity. Like you're inviting disaster to drop-kick you off a cliff.

It would be the most natural thing in the world for you to scale down your aspirations to something smaller. More realistic. Less scary. Which is totally okay. You have every right to be as you are and to live as you want to live.

All I'm saying is that life is on your side. Life loves you. It wants you to be successful.

Life's love for you may have escaped your notice if drama has dominated your days. It happens.

Look, I know life is on your side because you are here now. Somehow, you survived the challenges you've faced.

Give yourself credit. Countless people who went through something like what you have endured have given up by now.

Yet here you are, reading a book about creating a successful and satisfying business doing creative work you love. That proves you're magnificent. I'm proud of you.

You may have had a bumpy ride but look at the extraordinary person you have become in the process.

You may have had a bumpy ride but look at the extraordinary person you have become in the process.

You are already a winner. And you have more victories ahead of you. Because life has made you a person who has all she needs to succeed inside of her right now.

Fear of Success

While your conscious mind may passionately desire a thriving business, your unconscious mind may believe success should be avoided at all costs because something bad may happen.

Fear of success, like all fears, comes from feeling disconnected from something greater than yourself. If you let the fear dominate you, you feel even more disconnected.

Let's look at some of the most common limiting beliefs that block success. Notice whether any of these ideas resonate with you.

If my business is successful, it means I will …

- Lose control over my life, time, money, or energy
- Have to do things I don't want to do
- Be forced to give up something I value to pay for my success
- Have people leeching off of me until I have nothing left
- Become greedy, mean, or selfish
- Appear too intimidating to attract a romantic partner
- Make more money than I can handle, so I will end up losing every penny
- Have more freedom than I can handle, so I will do something foolish and bring shame on myself and my family
- Be held to an uncomfortably high standard of achievement, conduct, or income
- Lose my free time because I have to work every minute to stay on top
- Lose my privacy because everyone will know my business
- Never know if someone loves me just for myself
- Have to give everything until I have nothing left to give
- Be at risk of screwing it up and losing everything
- Lose my reason for living because once I've carried out my purpose there will be nothing left to live for

- Have wasted years feeling frustrated and miserable when this success was in my future all the time. All of my suffering will be for nothing.

Notice whether any of these concerns seem like valid reasons to avoid taking action to turn your dreams into bright, shiny reality.

Fortunately, most so-called downsides to success are misconceptions; secondhand opinions you accepted as gospel because they came from authority figures; or false conclusions, like "My rich uncle Dave worked himself to death"—blaming success for his demise when Scotch or sickness might have been the culprit.

The bottom line: You get to decide what success means to you. You define it. It does not define you.

You get to decide what success means to you.
You define it. It does not define you.

Fear of Failure

When you take on a big-ticket project like launching or expanding your creative business, it's natural to take the possibility of failure into account. Perhaps you worry that if your business goes under, you will:

- Disappoint yourself
- Let down loved ones
- Face financial ruin
- Feel bad, sad, or mad over having spent a lot of time, money, and energy for nothing

- Lose your last chance to escape the 9-to-5 rut, be your own boss, do something meaningful, get rich, prove yourself, share your gifts, or live your life purpose
- Have to endure embarrassment, shame, humiliation, or ridicule
- Anger or disappoint God

Worries like these are normal and legitimate, which makes it hard to talk yourself out of them.

They are real concerns. They can create real suffering. But they are not reality. Focusing on your fears increases the possibility that they will turn into reality because thoughts turn into things.

It serves you better to focus on what you want, rather than what you do not want. All thoughts are prayers, so it pays to be mindful about what you are praying for.

It serves you well to base your creative business on attractive energies like love and gratitude, rather than repelling energies like neediness or desperation.

It serves you best to anticipate success, satisfaction, and prosperity—and then get to work.

Waiting Until You Feel 100 Percent Confident Before Taking Action

You may be one of the many people who wait until they feel 100 percent confident before starting something new. In your case, launching or expanding your creative business.

This delay increases the odds that your company will never open its doors or reach its full potential. Waiting for 100 percent confidence involves a very looooong wait. A person could live her entire life without feeling completely confident.

Look, it's understandable to want to feel sure of your ability to make your dream business a reality before venturing forth.

And if you feel inadequate now, you naturally shrink from confirming your incompetence by trying and failing at something that means so much to you.

A hidden part of you may even worry that if your business tanks, you will have nothing left to hope for, or live for, if your most cherished dreams don't work out. So, it seems only logical, to your ego-mind, to refuse to venture at all rather than risk disaster.

The thing is, confidence comes *after* you take action, not before.

Many people have it backward. They want confidence first and then they'll take action.

It doesn't work that way.

Which is why waiting until you feel 100 percent confident before starting your dream business is a great way to ensure it will never happen.

In truth, if you're at least 51 percent confident that you can pull it off, you're good to go. Some levels of confidence can only be reached by taking action. It's impossible to think your way into a high degree of self-assurance; it must be earned through experience.

Fear of Making Mistakes

No one likes making mistakes. No one likes feeling foolish, inadequate, or ashamed. No one likes feeling as if they've wasted time, money, and energy on a failed enterprise.

So, if you're worried about making missteps as you go forward with your creative business, you have plenty of company.

That said, if you allow the fear of making mistakes to stop you—that is a mistake. Because you're holding your future hostage to your fears. You're making your doubts more important than your dreams, which grieves your soul. And when your soul ain't happy—ain't nobody happy.

When your soul ain't happy—
ain't nobody happy.

Remember this: mistakes are not real. They are not facts or actions or decisions. They are judgments you have made about certain facts, actions, and decisions. They have even less reality than a reality show.

"Mistake" is a meaning you have assigned to an experience. And you can change the meaning you give to an experience at any time.

You may have already done this without realizing it.

Let's say you once broke up with a man and then wished you hadn't. You see him ten years later and think, "I'm so glad we didn't end up together." A cause for regret at one point becomes an occasion for gratitude at another point. Yet, the past hasn't changed. The breakup still happened. You just changed your mind about whether it was a bad thing or a good thing.

You don't have to wait ten years to see a seeming error in a new light. To let go of blame or shame. To recognize the blessing or lesson in the experience.

You can call upon your Higher Power to give you right perception of the matter at any time, 24/7. Isn't it great to have Infinite Wisdom on tap?

Three Ways to See How Your Creativity Serves a Greater Good

Recognize How Your Creative Work Makes Life Better for Others

All work is sacred, including yours.

You bring beauty and order to the living or working environments of your clients when you serve as an interior designer, decorator, stylist, home décor maker or retailer, professional organizer, or Feng Shui practitioner. Your work also brings beauty and order to the hearts and minds of your people—making them happier, more peaceful and more productive. Everyone wins.

You make your clients look good and feel good when you serve as a fashion designer, seamstress, jewelry-maker, hair stylist, make-up artist, wedding planner, personal shopper, or stylist. Your clients pass on their good feelings to their loved ones and colleagues, creating more harmony in the home and in the workplace. And when your clients feel good, it opens the door for them to do good. Everyone wins.

You guide your clients to improved health and well-being when you serve as a personal trainer, nutritionist, fitness instructor, yogi, health coach, or medical intuitive. Enhancing your clients' physical health also strengthens their mental and emotional health, since they're all connected. This makes life better for your clients, as well as those who care about them. Everyone wins.

You help your clients build thriving companies that touch countless lives when you serve as a website designer, social media expert, content provider, SEO specialist, or business or marketing coach. Your clients' lives improve through higher income, financial peace of mind, and the joy of serving more people who want what they offer. The people your clients serve get their needs met. The economy perks up when your clients have more money to spend. Everyone wins.

You help clients lead their best lives when you serve as a life or business coach, speaker, nonfiction writer, intuitive healer, workshop facilitator, therapist, blogger, podcaster, or maker of instructional or inspirational videos. You empower your people to make positive changes in their lives. To do things smarter, faster, cheaper, or better. To understand themselves more deeply. You share know-how about life-enhancing skills that many of us would never learn if it weren't for you. Everyone wins.

You create a unique and compelling universe for your audience to dive into when you serve as a novelist, filmmaker, graphic novelist, cartoonist, videographer, singer, songwriter, or screenwriter. You conjure up characters and situations your followers care about or identify with, which makes them feel less alone. You take people on a journey where they may discover something, feel something, or just have a good time—all valid and valuable services. And it's a universe, a vision, a story only you can create. Everyone wins.

You help your audience see themselves and the world in a new light when you serve as a painter, sculptor, video-maker, graphic artist, photographer, scrapbooker, collage creator, or other kind of visual artist. You offer unique glimpses of beauty, emotion, drama, insight, deep feeling, and spiritual connection (or disconnection, as the case may be). Art widens our world. It touches our souls. Everyone wins.

You bring thrilling sights, sounds, thoughts, and feelings to your audience when you serve as a singer, dancer, actor, musician, or speaker. You bring the vibrancy of live performance to people hungry for human connection. Your energy revitalizes those who see you sharing your passion. You inspire dreams, insight, awe, wonder, and delight. You put yourself out there in all of your vulnerability, and we love you for it. Everyone wins.

You reconnect people with their best self or highest truth when you serve as a religious or spiritual counselor; a practitioner of intuitive or healing arts, such as Reiki; as a facilitator of creative, mystical, or transformational workshops, webinars, retreats, and meditations; as a reader of auras, energy, oracle cards, I Ching, numbers, sacred geometry, runes, Tarot, astrological charts, or cosmic forces; as a psychic or medium; or as an inspired tour guide to sacred sites. You tap into infinite intelligence, the quantum field, divine love, angels, the Akashic records, or other sources of timeless wisdom and bring it to people who wish to know more, be more, do more. Everyone wins.

All work is healing, including yours. Developing and sharing your creative talent does you a world of good. Your gifts bless others, too. Everyone wins.

Let Go and Let God

You will have days in your creative business when you're on fire with inspiration. When everyone thinks you're brilliant. When you feel gloriously unstoppable. Such days are to be treasured. Enjoy them.

You will have other days when a client asks for your guidance and then ignores it. When you've poured your heart and soul into creating an amazing service or product or work of art, and nobody wants it. When your creative muse pulls a no-show.

Such days can be discouraging. They can make you wonder whether you did the right thing in building a business around your creative gifts or make you doubt that you have any talent at all.

Which is why it would serve you well to unhook from your emotional attachment to the results of your efforts. It frees your heart and mind to focus on giving your best to the business you love.

Detaching from the outcome involves doing what is yours to do—the offer, the art, the book, the workshop, the video, the healing, the reading, the show—and then releasing it to the Universe.

You are only in charge of what you create. What happens once it's done is out of your hands.

I suggest that you learn to let go—not of control, but of the fantasy that you have control over the way other people respond to your offerings.

Two simple ways to let go and let God:

Bless everything to do with your business.

Bless the business itself. Bless yourself as a woman doing creative work.

Bless every one of your clients or customers, whether you find them adorable or aggravating.

Bless all of your emails before hitting "Send." Bless your website, those who designed it, and those who visit it. Bless your blog, newsletter, podcast, or YouTube channel. Bless all who subscribe to your list and all who are touched by your communications in any way.

Bless the place where you will give your talk or performance, bless those who fill the seats, bless your team, and bless your presentation.

Bless every dollar, euro, peso, or yen that comes your way.

Give thanks for everything to do with your business.

Give thanks for your creative business, whether it's going well or badly.

Offer gratitude to the one who gave you your creative talents.

Thank yourself for honoring your soul and the talents you have been given by creating a business around them.

Thank your people for the opportunity to serve them.

Express appreciation for every payment given to you.

Give thanks that you get to do work you love—and get paid for it.

Give thanks that you woke up today.

In the spirit of these suggestions, I say to you: Bless you for reading this book. May you find all the success and satisfaction you desire—and more. Thank you for being who you are and doing what you do.

Live Your Values

When you get clear about your values, it's easier to identify your priorities. Knowing your priorities simplifies your decision-making process. Having a quick and easy decision-making process saves you time, money, and energy. It also helps you sidestep the quagmire of self-doubt that keeps so many people stuck.

Determine what matters most to you and build that into your business. For instance, if you love to travel, make it part of what you offer: "Sign up 20 of your friends for this workshop and I will come to you." Make sure to price registration for the workshop high enough to cover your travel expenses, replace income lost by your absence from home base, and make a profit.

Clarity about your priorities helps you feel confident in saying "no" to opportunities that sound great but don't fit you.

For example, let's say your best friend wants you to join her new network marketing program. They sell vitamins, which dovetails with your primary work as a health coach or healer. But most network marketing gigs need your undivided attention if you want to make big money with them. They'll suck attention, time, and energy away from your creative work. Do you want to do that? Your own values will give you the answer. It also helps to remember that you make more money when you do something you enjoy.

Knowing your values helps you make the right call when it comes to deciding whether to take up a sideline, a volunteer opportunity, a day job, a joint venture, or your creative work.

Take a moment now to consider your values, such as:

Love	Compassion	Beauty
Order	Harmony	Integrity
Honor	Creativity	Generosity
Variety	Stability	Wealth

Wholeness	Completeness	Perfection
Wealth	Courage	Wisdom
Oneness	Peace	Strength
Passion	Family	Security
Consistency	Forgiveness	Clarity
Logic	Persistence	Serenity
Sexuality	Making a difference	Boldness
Acceptance	Humility	Grace
Religion	Fulfillment	Spirituality
Mother Earth	Holiness	Justice
Comfort	Curiosity	Work
Equality	Adventure	Fairness
Enlightenment	Expansion	The environment
Loyalty	Surrender	Fun
Art	Service	Contribution
Excellence	Nature	Community
Intelligence	Romance	Joy
Play	Invention	Poise
Calm	Principle	Achievement

When you have clarity about your values, incorporate them into a vision statement and a mission statement for your business.

A **vision statement** declares *why* you do what you do.

For instance, Religious Science Practitioners hold a vision of creating a world that works for everyone. Their vision statement might run along the lines of, "I am here to do my part in creating a world that works for everyone."

A **mission statement** tells *how* you do it.

To continue our example, Religious Science Practitioners may coach or counsel private clients, speak at events, conduct workshops, write articles or blog posts, create inspirational or instructional videos, offer seminars at sea, conduct tours of sacred sites, or run a podcast, among other possibilities. Their mission statement would note the specific services they offer to contribute toward creating a world that works for everyone.

Mission and vision statements show your people and prospects what you stand for.

They help you to remember what is important to you when you're considering a new project or opportunity.

And they ground your business in something greater than yourself, which gives your work more depth and meaning—heightening your sense of fulfillment in your day-to-day life.

How Marisol Found Her Calling

Marisol came to me because she felt bored and stuck after twenty years as a travel agent.

"I love setting up trips," she explained. "But I'm tired of being the one who sends people out on adventures, instead of having my own. I'm sick of sitting at a desk every day. I feel like life is passing me by—and I'm not getting any younger."

"What's stopping you from going on adventures right now?" I asked. "You know all the cool places to go and things to do."

"I'm scared," she admitted. "I feel stuck behind that desk, but I also feel safe there. I love the *idea* of traveling, and planning trips, but actual traveling is another story. Too many things can go wrong."

We talked about her interests, and Marisol shared that she's studied sacred sites around the world.

"I daydream about going to places like Sedona and Stonehenge," Marisol said. "I've been thinking a lot about Machu Picchu lately."

An ancient energy touched my awareness. "I'm sensing that the consciousness of Machu Picchu would like to talk with you right now. Is that okay?"

"Okay?" Marisol echoed. "Is it *possible*?"

"Well, yes. One thing I've found in this work is that if you can imagine

One thing I've found in this work is that
if you can imagine it, you can do it.

it, you can do it. Would you like to? It's like you've gotten an engraved invitation to talk to Machu Picchu, but it's okay to say no if you don't want to."

"I would love to talk with Machu Picchu!" she said. "This is amazing!"

I called upon Marisol's Higher Power to connect her consciousness with the consciousness of Machu Picchu, in the highest and best way for all concerned.

"I'm feeling it," she said after a few minutes. Her eyes filled. "It's calling me. It wants me to come."

Marisol took a deep breath. "I feel unworthy of this. Maybe it's a mistake. Machu Picchu probably wants someone else to come. Someone more important, or more spiritual, or something."

"If you feel called, it means someone is calling for you. If the calling was meant for someone else, you couldn't hear it." I paused. "Just so you know, it's okay to say no. You don't have to follow a calling. You have free will."

"But I want to go," Marisol protested. "More than anything. I didn't know it until a minute ago, but I do now. I feel it in my heart."

We focused the rest of the session on healing Marisol's feelings of unworthiness and increasing her faith in herself.

She emailed from Peru a few weeks later.

"I feel like I've come home," she wrote. "I never really felt like I belonged anywhere, but I belong here. I'm going to stay and study shamanism for two months. You've changed my life, Moira. Bless you."

I wrote back, "I'm thrilled for you! Please know how much I honor you for having the courage to follow your calling. You are amazing. Have a wonderful time!"

Marisol remains in Peru. She now leads shamanic healing journeys in and around Machu Picchu. They're booked out six months in advance.

You Can Do It, Too

Marisol came to me with what some call "divine discontent." Her life was okay, but she felt restless and bored. She wanted something more, yet understandably feared leaving her comfort zone—especially since she had no clear goal in mind.

She did not wake up one morning and say, "I want to be a shamanic healer in Peru." She just knew it was time for a change.

Inklings of a new direction came to Marisol in her daydreams of travel, but nothing specific. As often happens, her calling looked more like a tiny breadcrumb trail than a big red neon sign.

Our session gave her a first step—Machu Picchu asked Marisol to come and visit. She bravely accepted the invitation, and it led to another step, and then another.

It can work that way for you, too. You feel called to take one step. You take it, and it leads to the next step, which takes you to the step after that.

I encourage you to cultivate the flexibility to follow your calling, rather than insist that your path must take you in one specific direction or require that certain things must happen before you can be happy.

Sometimes you are the last person to know what will truly make you happy. You may not know it until you find it. Then your entire life makes sense, in retrospect. You see that every event and experience brought you to where you are meant to be. And from there, you move forward.

Your calling has come in the form of a strong desire to express ideas, images, stories, thoughts, or feelings in an artistic or intuitive way, like painting murals, or reading palms, or stepping in front of an open microphone at your local comedy club.

You wish you could spend more time pursuing your dreams and goals. If only you didn't have to deal with pesky practical details, like the rent or mortgage. You also like to eat on a regular basis, which would seem to eliminate the creative life as a real possibility for you.

The seeds of the solution lie in the problem. You can see them if you look at the matter from a different angle.

If you've been daydreaming about making a living doing what you love, but told yourself, "There's no way I can do that!"—turn it around.

Instead, ask yourself, "How *can* I do it? What is one thing I could do today to start making it happen?"

Your brain works like a Google search engine that operates at the speed of thought. You ask a question, and the answer comes to you from wherever it is. You only need to listen. If something isn't clear, you can say, "Can you explain that in a way I can understand?"

All the knowledge there is, is available to you. You just need to remember to ask. You can even ask for a sign.

All the knowledge there is, is available to you.
You just need to remember to ask.

A friend once told me, "I was driving around town, complaining to myself about something I really upset about, and I said out loud, 'Why me? Why is this happening to me?' Just then I stopped for a stoplight—right behind a truck that had a big sign on the back. It said, 'Why not?' I just burst out laughing. Why not, indeed? I was taking things too personally. I had a good laugh and felt much better. I don't even remember what I was upset about, but I remember 'Why not?'"

What you do with the information brought to you by signs, callings, and daydreams is up to you. You are free to act on it, or not. You can ask for details or alternatives, like, "What is a fun, easy way I could do that?"

Remember, your Higher Power wants for you what you want for yourself. You will never be given a dream without also being given the means to make it a reality.

You can ask for more information.

You can ask for help. It still counts as living your purpose if you accept assistance along the way.

You can ask for guidance and clarity whenever you want.

You were never meant to navigate this life alone. We all need each other. We are here to help, heal, teach, and learn with one another.

The way you serve is up to you.

If you want to do it by starting or expanding a business based on your creativity, hope and help are always just a thought away.

When you move toward your goal, the universe moves with you. Let it smooth the way. Let it light your path to the life, the love, the freedom and fulfillment you want.

Your success is waiting for you. It's time for you to meet it.

Afterword

"Work is love made visible."

—Kahlil Gibran

Creativity has been with us since the caveman days.

Hunters told stories about the lion that got away to an audience sitting spellbound around the campfire.

Artists dipped moss into red clay and used it to paint pictures of the tribe dancing, of horses running, of bison on the hoof.

Still others stitched together clothing, crafted arrowheads, fashioned ornaments, and set up altars to honor their gods.

Fast forward to today. Thanks to creativity, we can:

Live in a building. It could be a yurt, a Craftsman cottage, or a Malibu mansion. Without human imagination, we would still be living in caves.

Wear clothes, from ripped jeans to silky saris. Someone designed everything in your closet. (Heck, someone even designed your closet.) Others wove and dyed the fabric, stitched it together, displayed it in a way that made you want to buy it. Without creativity, what would we have to wear?

Travel to different places, using a car, a bike, a bus, a train, a plane, or a space shuttle. Someone conceived of every mechanical mode of transport we use. They got designed, built, and marketed in a way that appealed to you, so you use it. It could take days, months, or years to get from one place to another if it weren't for human creativity.

The world would poorer without:
Jane Eyre, Scarlett O'Hara, and Bridget Jones
Handheld computers, MRIs, and the Hubble Telescope
"Casablanca," "The Princess Bride," and "Love, Actually"
Social Security, National Health, and hospice

"Ode to Joy," "Somewhere Over the Rainbow," and "Born This Way"
Penicillin, aspirin, and the smallpox vaccine
Mickey Mouse, Bugs Bunny, and Hello Kitty
The Forbidden City, Versailles, and the Taj Mahal
"The Silent Spring," "The Feminine Mystique," and "I Know Why the Caged Bird Sings"
Chess, five-card stud, and Monopoly
Da Vinci's *Mona Lisa*, Picasso's *Guernica,* and Georgia O'Keefe's *Black Iris*
"Pride and Prejudice," "Wuthering Heights," and "Little Women"
Hagia Sophia, Angkor Wat, and Notre Dame
"I Love Lucy," "Game of Thrones," and "Jeopardy"
Lasagna, jalapeno cornbread, chocolate eclairs, and the ovens we use to bake them
All these blessings, and more, began in the imagination.

Despite creativity's undoubted contributions to humanity, it gets less credit than it deserves. It's regarded as entertaining but fundamentally frivolous and non-essential. It's something you do in your spare time. It's not considered real work.

Even you may underestimate the value of your artistry and imagination. Perhaps you question whether what you do has enough merit to justify charging people for it. Maybe you wonder how it can be right to make money from something you enjoy—isn't your paycheck supposed to be a reward for doing something boring, difficult, or unpleasant?

Consider this: the way Kahlil Gibran sees it, work is love made visible.

If that is true, your creative outpourings qualify as genuine work. They are real. And they matter. You are a member of the glorious tribe of humanity's creators, innovators, and visionaries.

You have only one precious life to live.

You can spend your days playing according to other people's rules, or you can make your own rules.

You can even throw out the rulebook altogether because, as far as the universe is concerned, there are no rules beyond cause and effect.

We're all just making up stuff as we go along. You might as well make up a life you love living.

A life that opens your heart. That fascinates your mind. Illuminates your spirit. And ignites your creative imagination.

A life in which you love your way to success, joy, and abundance of every kind.

I hold this vision for you until you can hold it for yourself, my friend.

Know that you are loved. You matter. You are wonderful exactly as you are. Bless you.

With love and appreciation,
Moira Shepard

Pick Up Your Free Confidence-Building Playbook

If you want to start turning your dream business into a successful and satisfying enterprise, get your free copy of "3 Power Moves to Share Your Gifts with the World: Your Confidence-Building Playbook."

The act of sharing your gifts creates a profound level of self-assurance. It builds dynamic confidence that carries you forward.

In this fun, easy guidebook you will find:

- The secret to building confidence you can count on
- Inspiration to get your creative juices flowing
- Fun, simple ways to get your gifts out there

Pick up your free guidebook to help you get on track—and stay there—at http://www.confidencebuildingplaybook.com today.

To your success!
Moira Shepard

Invitation to Connect

You are lovingly invited to get in touch with me.

Email: Moira@MoiraShepard.com

Web: https://www.MoiraShepard.com

Facebook: https://www.facebook.com/ConfidenceHereAndNow/

Twitter: http://www.twitter.com/Moira998

LinkedIn: http://www.linkedin.com/pub/moira-shepard/0/964/536